# Bill Zack

# TOMAHAWKED!

The Inside Story

of the Atlanta Braves'

Tumultuous Season

**Simon &
Schuster**

New York
London
Toronto
Sydney
Tokyo
Singapore

SIMON & SCHUSTER
Simon & Schuster Building
Rockefeller Center
1230 Avenue of the Americas
New York, New York 10020

Designed by H. J. Kim
Manufactured in the United States of America

10  9  8  7  6  5  4  3  2  1

Library of Congress Cataloging-in-Publication Data
Zack, Bill.
    Tomahawked! : the inside story of the Atlanta Braves'
tumultuous season / Bill Zack.
        p.   cm.
    1.  Atlanta Braves (Baseball team)   I.  Title.
GV875.A8Z33.   1993
796.357'64'09758231—dc20                           93-47
                                                    CIP

ISBN: 0-671-86878-0

Photo Credits

Courtesy of the Atlanta Braves, 10; Scott Cunningham
Photography, 1, 2, 3, 4, 5, 6, 7, 8, 9, 11, 12, 13, 16, 17, 18, 19,
20; Photos by Joe Sebo, 14, 15.

# Dedication

For Jane Hardacre Zack, mother and friend.
She knew.

# Acknowledgments

Like the Braves, who unlimbered in the warmth of West Palm Beach last March and dreamed of returning to the World Series, I began this project with no inkling of what the future held. If the season unfolded as it had in 1991, with the team repeating as National League champions, I hoped a book would follow, but there were no guarantees. Thus, I'm grateful to my agent, Shari Wenk, who encouraged me to keep writing, even as the Braves got off to a slow start and nearly sank out of sight in May. I'm indebted to my editor at Simon & Schuster, Jeff Neuman, for taking a chance on a first-time author. He cares about writers and their work and for that I'm thankful. I owe words of gratitude to Bill Plaschke of the *Los Angeles Times* and author John Feinstein for their advice and encouragement. I would also like to thank Jim Schultz and the Braves public relations department for all their help. A special thank-you goes to my wife, Ann, whose patience and understanding during this project was above and beyond the call of duty. She's the only woman I'd wear a ring for.

Last, a few words about the players. I have been covering the Braves since 1987, and during that time I have come to recognize the game of baseball as practiced in the major leagues is not the same game that was played on the sandlots of my childhood. It is first and foremost a business. The pressure to reach the majors is unyielding; the pressure to remain there is unforgiving. A major league baseball team brings together a diverse group of players and demands that they spend seven months together in close quarters. As in any large family, there is bound to be quarreling among some members, as well as disappointment and bitterness among others. That was certainly true of the Braves during the 1992 season. Yet, through it all, they remained gentlemen. I doubt you will find any players with more class than Terry Pendleton, Tom Glavine, Charlie Leibrandt, Greg Olson, Otis Nixon, Kent Mercker, Sid Bream, Mike Stanton, and Mark Lemke. No player is funnier than Jeff Blauser or more cooperative than John Smoltz. Sitting in the dugout and talking with Bobby Cox and his coaches hours before the stadium gates open remains a favorite part of my job. Prying information from John Schuerholz remains one of life's great challenges.

I owe my thanks to all the Braves for their patience and understanding.

# OCTOBER 1991

**Mark Lemke** watched the crowd swarm past police barricades and engulf Atlanta's Peachtree Street in a surging sea of tomahawks and Braves caps, and he wondered to himself what the celebration would have been like if the team had *won* the World Series.

Three days after the Series ended in heartbreak fashion for the Braves, a 1–0 loss in 10 innings to the Minnesota Twins in Game Seven, the team gathered a final time to say good-bye to their fans. Dressed in coats and ties, they looked out of place amid the skyscrapers and asphalt, though the sounds of war chants and throbbing tom-toms spilling across the cool fall air made them feel at home.

There was Terry Pendleton, the veteran third baseman who started every game from June 15 until the team clinched the division title, despite being hobbled by a cartilage tear in his left knee. And Ron Gant, the muscular center fielder who had joined the ranks of the game's premier players with another dominant season, and pitchers Tom Glavine and Steve Avery, who had combined to form the most potent one-two punch in the league.

A convoy of convertibles waited to sweep them down Peachtree and into a busy winter. Lemke, the dwarfish second baseman who had seen the Series Most Valuable Player Award slip away from him when Twins pitcher Jack Morris pitched all 10 innings in the finale, was anxious to get going. Catcher Greg Olson, who had spent seven and a half years toiling in the minor leagues before he reached the majors, was eager to return to his native Minnesota and pursue his long-delayed passion: hunting. Pitcher John Smoltz, who had leaped happily into Olson's arms after the team clinched the division title, then again after winning Game Seven of the National League Championship Series, was eager for the off-season to begin for another reason. His wife, Dyan, was eight months pregnant with their first child.

Yet no one really wanted it to end. It had been a season the Braves and their fans would never forget. In six months the team had transformed a city *Sports Illustrated* dubbed "Losersville" into a metropolis of frenzied, tomahawk-chopping, war-whooping baseball fanatics.

There had never been anything like it in Braves history. Not even the "Miracle Braves" of 1914, the Boston team that climbed out of the cellar in July to win the National League pennant, then swept Connie Mack's Philadelphia Athletics in four games in the World Series, could rival this miracle.

In the 25 years since the franchise had moved from Milwaukee to Atlanta, the Braves had won just two National League West titles and had lost both playoff series in three straight games. Legendary players like Hank Aaron, Eddie Mathews, and Phil Niekro had never brought the city a World Series.

Now, having completed the most unlikely season in baseball history—a wondrous turnaround from last place to first place in a single year—Braves fans rejoiced. Pandemonium reigned on Peachtree. Fans began to gather even before police officers arrived, climbing buildings, billboards, and trees, and stacked 30 and 40 deep on the sidewalks. By the time the parade began, with Atlanta mayor Maynard H. Jackson in the lead convertible, 750,000 fans had collected along the one-

and-a-half-mile route, the largest gathering in the city's history.

The police were woefully unprepared for the onslaught. Five hundred officers patrolled the route; another 500 were needed. As Lemke's convertible headed down Peachtree, the crowd poured over the barricades, ignoring officers' pleas to return to the sidewalks, and hurled themselves at their heroes.

"This is getting a little rough," an alarmed Lemke shouted above the pandemonium.

Unrestrained, fans pawed at the players, seeking a handshake or an autograph. Hands reached at the players, ripping off buttons and tugging at sleeves. Outfielder Deion Sanders, who would return to his second career as a defensive back with the Atlanta Falcons following the parade, clenched a fist as people swarmed toward him. He wasn't being violent, he explained later; it was "just so they wouldn't take my rings off."

Along different parts of the parade route, other players were experiencing similar problems. A fan climbed onto pitcher Mike Stanton's car before he was removed.

"I almost lost my arm a couple of times," Stanton said. "Really, what I was trying to do was keep them off my wife."

Outfielder Tommy Gregg lost a button on his sportcoat as fans reached toward him.

"They were climbing over me to get to [first baseman] Brian Hunter," Gregg said. "That made me feel real good."

Slowly the procession moved down Peachtree as ticker tape sprinkled the players and applause thundered in their ears. They waved and saluted until their arms ached. People clogged the streets, forcing the marching bands to troop along in single file.

"It was like they only wanted to touch us," marveled first baseman Sid Bream. "Once they did, everything was fine."

Lemke was almost pulled from his convertible as he shook outstretched hands.

"It was like a rock concert," he would say later. "A touch of a hand would make someone faint."

Everywhere Lemke looked, tomahawks waved madly, children playing hooky from school squealed with excitement, and businessmen in gray suits shouted and waved.

"The sheer number of people took your breath away," he said, shaking his head.

A much-maligned city, without a sports champion among its three major teams in its history, was having the time of its life. Raising his voice to be heard above the din, Gant exclaimed, "This is just the beginning of something that is going to be good for a long, long time."

For general manager John Schuerholz, who had completed the rebuilding of the team by signing Pendleton, Bream, left fielder Otis Nixon, reliever Juan Berenguer, and shortstop Rafael Belliard as free agents the previous winter, the parade was the sweetest moment of his life. Although he had won a world championship with the 1985 Kansas City Royals, Schuerholz was staggered by the sudden success of the Braves in his first year with the organization. Looking at the team during spring training, he had hoped they could climb two or three places and perhaps finish with a .500 record, a respectable showing for a club that had lost 97 games in 1990.

A studious, intense man who once taught geography in Baltimore's public school system, Schuerholz figured in another year the team could begin to challenge the Los Angeles Dodgers and Cincinnati Reds. Now, riding in one of the lead convertibles with his wife, Karen, and son Jonathan, he raised his eyes and watched the ticker tape descend and grinned like a lottery winner.

"It was one of the more joyous moments in my life," he reflected later. "It was like a dream sequence, like the whole community had come out to shower their emotions on us. It was overwhelming, it really was."

How different his emotions had been three days before. Just after the Series ended, Schuerholz sat alone in the first-class section of the Braves' chartered plane at Minneapolis–St. Paul International Airport, his face drawn and his eyes glistening.

"We had the brass ring right in our hands," he said mournfully, "and they ripped it right out."

The flight back to Atlanta was subdued. The cabins were festooned with crepe paper and balloons, and trays of hors d'oeuvres were passed along each row, but no one felt like eating. Manager Bobby Cox, who had endured five lonely seasons as the club's general manager before returning to the dugout, moved slowly along the aisles, shaking hands and murmuring words of encouragement. He could read the hurt in the eyes of outfielder Lonnie Smith, who had blundered on the bases in the eighth inning of Game Seven, and see the disappointment on the face of Smoltz, who had worked eight gritty innings and not allowed a run.

Cox walked on and the players talked quietly, consoling each other, then tilted their seats back and closed their eyes.

The plane touched down at Atlanta's Hartsfield Airport two hours later. As it taxied toward the terminal, Hunter, the rookie first baseman, wondered aloud whether any fans would be on hand to greet the team.

It was 4:30 A.M.

Gathering their bags, players trooped wearily into a reception area and were stunned to see several thousand people waving banners and pennants, whooping and hollering at them.

Smoltz, raising his voice above the uproar, said, "It's just what we needed after a loss like that."

Now, three days later, another tumultuous greeting was stunning the team. As the parade wound down and players gathered at the City Hall annex, Olson wove his way through the crowd and spotted Gant near the podium. Clasping his shoulder and squeezing his hand, Olson smiled and said, "I thought I might miss you and I just wanted to tell you it's been great."

As their eyes met and locked, Gant answered quietly, "And it will be great next year."

# MARCH

In 1991 they were baseball's little darlings, a team of kids, castoffs, rejects, and underachievers, the league's doormat rising to contend, then conquer. Everybody loves a spunky underdog, and the Braves fit the bill, a real-life Rocky knocking off the contenders to reach the title match.

Now, almost four months after Gene Larkin's fly sailed over left fielder Brian Hunter's head, ending Game Seven of the World Series in the tenth inning, the question facing the Braves was: Could they do it again?

Preparing to head to the team's spring training headquarters in West Palm Beach, Florida, Mark Lemke thought about how different the 1992 season would be, how Braves fans would expect more from the club and opposing teams would relish the thought of knocking off the defending champs.

"It's definitely going to be a different type of atmosphere for us," he said. "There are great expectations for us, but we've just got to try and block that out and play the same way we've always played."

It was a strange feeling for the Braves to hold any expectations at all. This team had spent much of the previous decade as the laughingstock of baseball, an organization so inept that owner Ted Turner once donned a uniform and moved into the dugout to manage the team for one game: He lost. The Braves would try anything—except winning—to draw fans into Atlanta–Fulton County Stadium. They sponsored ostrich races and wet T-shirt contests. They hired famed highwire artist Karl Wallenda to perform. (After crossing the stadium 100 feet above the ground, he headed to the press lounge, where he quickly downed a couple of double-strength martinis.) They even sponsored Headlock & Wedlock Night, in which 50 couples were married before the game—moving down an aisle formed by players holding bats—and pro wrestling was offered afterward. The Braves were baseball's circus, Turner was their ringmaster, and baseball guffawed as it looked on.

Turner's wild gimmicks couldn't cover up the team's incompetence. In the 17 years since he bought the club, it had finished with a losing record 13 times. All the dancing girls on dugouts, silly costumed characters, and putty-faced pitchmen he used to attract fans could not distract from the truth: The Braves were baseball's worst franchise and no amount of hype and glitter would make a difference. Turner finally realized his folly and stowed away his "Captain Outrageous" costume, eased back into the TBS boardroom, and turned the baseball operation over to team president Stan Kasten and Bobby Cox, whom he brought aboard as general manager in 1985, after having fired him as field manager four years before.

In slow, measured steps, Cox rebuilt the barren farm system. Much of the foundation had been laid before he arrived. To the nucleus of Glavine, David Justice, Lemke, Jeff Blauser, and Gant he added Avery, Stanton, Kent Mercker, and Mark Wohlers through the draft, and he traded Doyle Alexander to the Detroit Tigers for Smoltz. However, even with this young talent moving up through the minor leagues, it would be five years before the organization turned a corner. In the meantime the Braves continued to be one of baseball's worst teams, a sad collection of players who would lose 106 games in 1988, then drop 97 games in each of the next two seasons.

So many players passed through the clubhouse in those years that a turnstile should have been installed at the entrance. It seemed every time the Braves made a move it backfired. They gave $10 million to reliever Bruce Sutter and he blew out his shoulder. Steve Bedrosian was traded away to the Phillies and he won a Cy Young Award there. Atlanta's favorite son, Dale Murphy, was also traded to the Phils, but not before his play had slipped so badly that the Braves could get only three mediocre players in return for the two-time MVP. First baseman Nick Esasky was hired away from the Boston Red Sox and soon developed a severe case of vertigo that ended his career after just 35 at-bats in a Braves uniform.

Fans steered wide of the stadium. While baseball's popularity soared elsewhere, the Braves drew fewer than one million fans in three straight seasons, an embarrassing slight for a team that had left behind tremendous fan support in Milwaukee in search of supposedly greener pastures in the Southeast. When Schuerholz arrived he found an organization with little of its pride remaining, a dispirited and melancholy group huddled in the tiny offices of a graying hulk of a stadium. Nattily dressed and impeccably groomed, he projected the image of a highly successful businessman, a dynamic, energetic man who had spent 23 years helping to build the Royals into one of baseball's most successful franchises. His hiring was a coup for Kasten, who lured him away with a million-dollar contract and the promise to let him run things his own way. Vowing to turn the Braves into the "Royals of the South," he began by focusing on the defense. He lavished a $10 million contract on Terry Pendleton, a staggering deal for a player beset by injuries and coming off a .230 season in St. Louis. He gave Sid Bream $5.6 million to leave Pittsburgh. Next, he signed Rafael Belliard, a backup shortstop for the Pirates, then added Juan Berenguer from the Twins and catcher Mike Heath from the Tigers. By the time he was through, Schuerholz had committed $25 million to rebuilding the Braves, and many observers felt the best he had done was buy himself a .500 team. How wrong they were. The pitching staff benefited from the improved defense, and Pendleton shocked his former employers in St. Louis by emerging as one of the league's best players. By the end of Schuerholz's first year on the job the Braves had written one of baseball's best stories, rising from last place to first and playing in a World Series.

However, with the team's success came new problems. While Pendleton and Bream were tied up with multiyear deals, most of the other players negotiated new contracts every year and a growing number had arbitration rights. Schuerholz had begun spending Turner's money at a dizzying pace, eating up much of the $7 million profit the club posted in 1991 with hefty pay hikes to a half-dozen players. Glavine wound up with a $2.9 million salary, up from $722,000, while Gant and Alejandro Pena each agreed to salaries of $2.65 million, raises of $1.45 million and $1.65 million, respectively. After testing the free agent market, Otis Nixon returned for $2.7 million per year; he had made $585,000 in '91. Salaries were climbing so quickly that Schuerholz figured the team's payroll would shoot from $19 million in 1991 to $34 million this season and would pass $40 million by 1993.

"We're kind of in a new galaxy of salaries and we're going in at warp speed," he said.

Spending money on the Braves had never bothered Turner, who was listed among the world's wealthiest people by *Forbes*, with his net worth judged at $2 billion. While he ran Turner Broadcasting with the aggressive and ruthless style of a corporate raider, his baseball team was handled with a parental touch. Even as he began to distance himself from the daily operation of the team, he continued to okay multi-million-dollar contracts for free agents, though very few of them panned out.

Schuerholz had free rein to spend Turner's money as he wanted, but he still had to operate on a prudent business basis. In the ever-escalating economic world of baseball salaries, that meant holding the line against younger players, those in the first three years of their major league career who did not qualify for salary arbitration. Without those rights, they had no alternative but to ultimately accept the club's offer, though the policy always caused hard feelings between the players and the front office. Last year Smoltz had become so irritated at the club's refusal to up its offer to him that he walked out of spring training for two days.

It was Justice who got upset this spring. He was angered by the team's first offer of $400,000, a raise of little more than $100,000, while Avery was disappointed his 18-win season and MVP Award in the National League Championship Series did not result in an offer of more than $300,000.

Justice was seething when he arrived in Florida. He and his agent, Eric Goldschmidt, who also handled Los Angeles Dodgers stars Eric Davis and Darryl Strawberry, wanted a one-year deal for $600,000, while Schuerholz remained adamant about signing him for less than $500,000. Without the leverage of arbitration rights, Goldschmidt and Justice were at Schuerholz's mercy because he could cut salaries by up to 20 percent if he chose to. Their only recourse was to complain publicly, and their only real threat was to walk out of camp.

Justice, whose outspoken and brash nature often irritated his teammates, could not wait to unload on the Braves. He had barely dropped his duffel bag on the clubhouse floor when he launched the first salvo.

"I'm unhappy with my contract," he said. "It's not fair. I feel I should be at the top of my class by a bunch. None of the others carry the responsibility that I do."

Justice had a point. At age 25, with barely two major league seasons under his belt, he was the club's cleanup hitter and a budding superstar. The Braves had discovered what he meant to the lineup last season when he missed two months with a back injury. Without him, they were 28–20. When he returned, he hit 10 home runs and collected 36 RBI and the team went 31–14. The Braves could not do without him and he knew it.

But his attitude didn't help matters, either with his teammates or with the front office. He had turned off many players the previous spring when he arrived in camp driving a Mercedes with a vanity license plate that read "Sweet Swing," the first of several incidents that had left him with a reputation for being arrogant and egotistical. Justice is a handsome, intelligent, and articulate man, one who draws all eyes when he enters a room, and a player who plays the game with a rare grace. He was supremely confident of his ability from the first moment he stepped into the Braves clubhouse as a rookie, and many of the Braves felt he was cocky and brash. He had not formed many close friendships on the team, which caused many players to feel he was aloof and not a good teammate, and it didn't enhance his image when rumors reached the clubhouse the previous year that he had been spotted dancing in an Atlanta nightclub while he was injured and the team was on a road trip.

Avery was almost as angry about his contract as Justice. Quiet and shy, and still only 21, he had just a season and a half in the big leagues under his belt and had to make the rounds of card shows and television shopping network appearances during the winter to supplement his income. Now that it was time for them to pay up, he felt the Braves were refusing to reward him for his outstanding season. Seated at his locker in the Municipal Stadium clubhouse in West Palm Beach, Avery's baby face was stern and his voice was low and threatening.

"I don't think Ted Turner would want his team run this way," he said. "I don't think he realizes what they're doing. I won't let it affect my performance, but I won't forget it. They think I won't remember it when it comes time for salary arbitration and free agency, but I will."

Unlike Avery, Justice did allow his unresolved contract to affect his performance. He went off to the side during morning exercises to follow his own program and he loafed during outfield drills. Cox approached Pendleton, whom he viewed as the unofficial team captain, and asked him to have a word with Justice.

Later, in a deserted clubhouse, Pendleton pulled Justice into a corner and laid down the law.

"David, you won't be allowed to disrupt this team," Pendleton told him. "You and I will come to blows before that happens. When you want to apply yourself, you can have more impact than anyone else here. You're a very talented player. Stop separating yourself and join the team."

Justice listened and had little response. Later, Pendleton admitted he wasn't sure if he had gotten through to him, and there was no immediate change in Justice's actions on the field.

While Avery knew he had no alternative except to keep negotiating with the Braves in hopes of reaching a compromise, Justice and Goldschmidt had other ideas. They schemed to back Schuerholz into a corner and force a showdown. Their plan started with Photo Day, an annual shoot for card company photographers, news organizations, and others to photograph players individually. While his teammates posed in front of the cameras, Justice refused to participate, and Goldschmidt informed Schuerholz his client wouldn't do anything for the team except play baseball until his contract demands were met.

Schuerholz was appalled. "If David was my son, he wouldn't act this way," he said. "If he doesn't want to act like a member of the team, if he doesn't want to be shoulder to shoulder with his teammates, that is entirely his choice."

A diminutive man with the boyish face of a high school freshman, Goldschmidt reveled in the rough-and-tumble world of high-stakes negotiating. Once a certified public accountant in Beverly Hills, he had become one of baseball's best-known agents by demanding from clubs, then delivering to his clients, outrageous contracts that had helped escalate the game's salaries at a phenomenal rate. As the deadline approached to settle contracts, Goldschmidt met privately with Schuerholz and delivered an ultimatum: Either the Braves up their offer to $555,000, he told Schuerholz, or Justice would refuse to participate in any club-related activities during the season, except to play baseball.

"David has provided the Braves with a lot of free services off the field," Goldschmidt said. "This is a way to demonstrate to the Braves that the contract is not fair."

Seated in a plush trailer that served as the club's front office headquarters during spring training, Schuerholz pondered the situation. He couldn't allow Justice to disrupt the team, yet he couldn't be seen to be caving in to Goldschmidt's demands. He could trade Justice, but the fans in Atlanta would hang him in effigy if he did, then tar and feather him and run him out of town on a rail. He could ignore Goldschmidt's threats, but he sensed the little man wasn't bluffing.

Several hours before the deadline, Goldschmidt sat in the first row of seats at Municipal Stadium, next to the home dugout, basking in the Florida sunshine. He was relaxed and confident that Schuerholz would retreat during a meeting scheduled for later in the day. Sure enough, when Justice and Goldschmidt sat down with the general manager, he upped his offer to $555,000 and an uneasy truce was signed. Justice accepted the deal and pledged he would cooperate in all the team's activities, including posing later in the spring during another photo shoot.

He was ecstatic that he got what he wanted, but was puzzled by the club's willingness to stiff him right up until the end.

"What upsets me the most is what I've had to go through to get a good contract," he said. "You would have thought it would have been easier this year after the World Series. If we were coming off a last-place finish, I could understand fighting for money."

Schuerholz upped his offer to Avery to $355,000 just before the deadline and he accepted, though, like Justice, he didn't understand why the Braves haggled over a relatively small amount of money.

"I would have had a hard time forgetting about all this if I would have gotten just three hundred and ten thousand dollars," he said. "Now I can just go on and play baseball."

. . .

An encore to the miracle season, Schuerholz knew, would be the real test of his abilities. As the team prepared for its first spring exhibition game, he had made no significant moves to improve the club, even as the Reds and Dodgers, who figured to be the Braves' primary competition in the National League West, dramatically reshaped themselves. There was one deal he was interested in, but he didn't feel confident he could pull it off. The Pirates were willing to trade left fielder and 1990 MVP Barry Bonds because they couldn't afford to pay him what he wanted—a five-year contract in the $25–$30 million range. Schuerholz felt Bonds was the best player in the league, but he wasn't sure he could meet Pirates general manager Ted Simmons's asking price of several players in return. In addition, he knew he would have to sign Bonds to a long-term deal, then trade Nixon to make room for him in the outfield. He discussed the deal with Simmons again and again, revising the players who would be included each time. Names were hurled around—Brian Hunter, Kent Mercker, Alejandro Pena, Mark Wohlers, Keith Mitchell—and Simmons, on the job for less than three months, was certain a deal could be worked out.

"We were very close," Simmons would say later. "I thought we were going to get it done, I really did."

While he continued his talks with Simmons, Schuerholz was also on the phone with California Angels general manager Whitey Herzog, setting up a deal for Nixon. Herzog was desperately seeking a leadoff hitter and had wooed Nixon with a $5 million offer at the winter meetings, only to be rebuffed when the outfielder re-signed with the Braves. Schuerholz was reluctant to part with Nixon, who gave the team its first true leadoff hitter since Brett Butler was dealt to Cleveland in 1983, but he had little choice. There would be no room for Nixon in an outfield of Bonds, Justice, and Gant.

Nixon was dismayed to hear his name mentioned in trade talks. After a tumultuous winter he had returned to the Braves, partly out of a sense of loyalty to his teammates, whom he felt he owed after being suspended for drug use in the middle of last September's pennant race. He had come to the Braves in an April 1991 trade with the Expos, a speedy outfielder with a can't-hit reputation, and had become one of those unlikely success stories baseball seems to produce every year. At age 32, he had emerged as one of the league's most dangerous leadoff men by hitting .297 and shattering the franchise record with 72 stolen bases. It was Nixon who set the tone for an offense that scored the second-most runs in the league, giving it a dimension it had long lacked by disrupting pitchers and infielders with his speed. However, lurking behind his confident smile and quiet nature was a tormented soul. Nixon had used cocaine before and he would use it again, and when a drug test revealed his problem, he fled, leaving his teammates stunned.

The Braves had a game-and-a-half lead over the Dodgers with 19 games remaining on September 16 when Nixon was suspended by the commissioner's office. The announcement shocked the Braves, most of whom didn't know Nixon had used drugs in the past.

"It left me with a sickening feeling in my stomach," Deion Sanders said later.

Dressed in black and wearing sunglasses, Nixon strode through San Francisco International Airport that afternoon clutching an airline ticket and a small travel bag. The Braves would not hear from him until he released a statement four days later.

"I want to apologize to my teammates, the fans, and the kids for letting them down at this time," he wrote. "It is tough for me right now, but I have made the right decisions and the problem and situations at hand are being dealt with. I would like the team to continue winning and concentrating on the pennant. I know they will get the job done."

Since a drug-related incident in Cleveland in 1987, Nixon had been tested over 200 times by the commissioner's office and been found clean. Only later, as the Braves were recovering from the shock of his suspension, would it be revealed that Nixon had failed a drug test in July 1991. He and his agent, Joe Sroba, had argued at the time that the test was incorrect, and the commissioner's office had relented and allowed him to continue playing.

Following his suspension Nixon returned to Atlanta and entered a drug treatment center, emerging just long enough in December to sign his new two-year contract, with an option for a third year, a deal that could net him over $8 million. His signing had not been endorsed wholeheartedly by either fans or the media. The Braves had been criticized for sending out the wrong message when they rehired Nixon, rewarding a drug user who had failed himself and his teammates when they needed him the most. Nixon had deflected the controversy by speaking openly about his addiction and had promised to finance a drug awareness film aimed at kids.

Unsure how fans would respond to him in spring training, Nixon had begun a low-key campaign in January to regain their support. He had granted one interview and used Atlanta's largest newspaper—the *Journal-Constitution*—to get his message out. He described his addiction as a disease, apologized for letting down the team and its fans, and asked for forgiveness. It seemed to have worked.

"Going through what I went through I wouldn't wish on any man," he said. "I turned my life, and all this stuff that was going on during a certain period of time, to God. There is where I'm at with myself today. [God] is sort of running things. I had dropped the ball in trying to lead my life around. Now God is in control of what is going on with the situation. This is [His] will, to share this story with people."

When spring training opened he was warmly embraced by his teammates, who treated him as if nothing had happened, and fans were kind to him from the moment he first stepped from the dugout. He seemed the same old Nixon and made no secret of the commissioner's office testing him for drugs several times a week, or of his enrollment in a support group for addicts. He had straightened out his life and though he would miss the first three weeks of the season as he finished serving his suspension, he was happy to be back with the

Braves. The rumored deal with the Angels caught him off-guard. He was hurt that Schuerholz would consider trading him just two months after signing him, and he wondered if he had been wrong in rejecting Herzog's offer.

"If Schuerholz doesn't want me, why did he re-sign me?" Nixon asked.

In this instance, Schuerholz was like a little kid in a toy store, who saw a toy he liked on one aisle, then turned a corner and spotted another toy he liked twice as much. In Bonds he saw a player with the rare combination of speed and power, a player who would give the Braves the league's most fearsome lineup, and he was determined to do all he could to have him. Most players didn't share Schuerholz's eagerness to add Bonds to the team. The reaction inside the clubhouse to news of the proposed trade was one-sided: Nobody wanted him. Bonds was regarded as a malcontent and a negative clubhouse presence and the feeling was unanimous among the Braves. "Why spoil a good thing?" several players wondered.

One player looked across the room at Justice and said, "Can you imagine having the two biggest assholes in baseball on the same team?"

Another player flatly stated, "We don't want him."

Yet Schuerholz was dogged in his pursuit. He and Simmons talked every day, sometimes several times a day, but each man was unwilling to compromise on the players to be included in the trade. Schuerholz knew Simmons was under pressure to get rid of Bonds, who could leave Pittsburgh at the end of the season as a free agent. With two other big-money contracts looming, for center fielder Andy Van Slyke and pitcher Doug Drabek, Simmons simply couldn't afford Bonds. Schuerholz wanted Bonds badly, but he didn't want to give up two or three of his best young prospects to get him.

In Bradenton, Florida, where the Pirates train, Bonds was excited about the possibility of playing for the Braves.

"If I was in Atlanta I think I might go thirty-thirty [home runs and steals] every year," he said. "Playing eighty-one times in Atlanta . . . whew."

Once word of the possible deal leaked out, Schuerholz and Simmons were besieged by the media. Their phones jangled all day, they were hounded by questions wherever they went, and no matter how often they insisted no deal was imminent, trade talk was the top story each day. Simmons attempted to end the constant stream of rumors being printed in Atlanta and Pittsburgh newspapers by saying, "The names are out there. Is the deal imminent? No. Have we come to an understanding [with the Braves]? No. Right now I perceive my outfield on Opening Day will include Barry Bonds."

Behind the scenes, Schuerholz and Simmons worked diligently to strike a deal. On March 19, the two men finally agreed to a two-for-one swap, Bonds for Pena and Mitchell, a young outfielder. That evening, during a telephone conversation, they reconfirmed the deal and agreed to talk again the next day to wrap up the technicalities.

When Schuerholz reached his office at Municipal Stadium the next morning he had a message waiting for him from Simmons. His heart sank as he read the terse memo calling off the deal.

"What happened?" he wondered. "We had a done deal."

In Bradenton, Pirates manager Jim Leyland had become increasingly worried about losing his left fielder. Having already lost right fielder Bobby Bonilla, one of baseball's top sluggers, to free agency during the winter, he didn't want to see his best run producer depart. During a meeting with Simmons the night before, a few hours after the general manager had confirmed the deal with Schuerholz, Leyland asked Simmons not to trade Bonds. Reluctantly, he agreed, and the next day he announced that "under no circumstances will Barry Bonds be traded."

Bonds was unhappy the deal had collapsed. As usual, he was loud and oblivious to the feelings of his teammates in expressing his displeasure.

"I'd love to go to Atlanta," he said. "I'll play for any of the California teams, either of the New York or Chicago teams or Atlanta . . . because they have a chance to win for a long time. That's my biggest goal of all, to get a World Series ring. I think my best chance of that would be in Atlanta."


While attention in the Braves camp centered on Bonds, several players quietly expressed unhappiness with their own situations. Second baseman Jeff Treadway had read his name in trade stories all winter and wondered if he would be with the team when it broke camp in six weeks, while shortstop Jeff Blauser had become tired of his backup role and wanted a regular spot in the lineup.

Treadway grew up in Griffin, Georgia, about 40 miles south of Atlanta, and played college ball at the University of Georgia, then was signed by the Cincinnati Reds. He never got a chance to play with the Reds because they had second baseman Ron Oester ahead of him, so he was delighted when then-Cincinnati general manager Murray Cook gave him away to the Braves for $50,000 in March of 1989.

Treadway and the Braves were a perfect fit. He returned home where he felt most comfortable, and the team received a player who would blossom into one of the best offensive second basemen in the game. Though only an average defensive player, he is a dangerous left-handed hitter who hit 11 homers and collected 59 RBIs in 1990. Hampered by a sore right hand during the latter part of last season, his power had vanished, but he still led the team in hitting with a .320 average.

Now he wondered to himself if the trade rumors were true. Although Lemke was the superior defensive player and frequently replaced him late in games, he couldn't match Treadway's offensive skills. Lemke's career average was .225 and there was no way he could handle the number two slot in the order behind Otis Nixon, yet the Braves seemed ready to give him the job.

Treadway thought his dream world was crumbling. The team had signed infielder/outfielder Steve Lyons as a free agent in January, figuring he could back up Lemke and Pendleton, a plan that left no room for Treadway. Hoping for a show of support from Cox, Treadway was disappointed. Cox refused to say Lemke was his starter, but he wouldn't reject the idea either.

"I'm a little bit surprised by the willingness of the Braves to go ahead and do something with me," Treadway said. "I know the times I've been out there playing every day I've been productive. I'm taking the attitude that if I'm traded somebody is going to be very happy to get me."

The Braves had shopped Treadway for a couple of years without finding an attractive offer. The word on baseball's grapevine is that teams playing on artificial turf don't want him because his lack of range would allow too many ground balls to speed through the infield, while other teams were leery of the club's asking price of a top prospect in return. But before Schuerholz could make a deal, the decision was taken out of his hands. Treadway's hand began to bother him again. This raised the eyebrows of Cox and his coaching staff. They wondered why he hadn't had surgery during the winter and found it a little too convenient that as trade rumors begin to swirl faster, Treadway's hand began to ache.

Treadway knew what was being said, but he shrugged away the criticism. On doctor's orders he hadn't picked up a bat during the winter, hoping the injury would heal without the need for an operation. After three months of inactivity, he came to camp pain-free and was confident the problem wouldn't resurface. The strategy collapsed, however, as soon as he picked up a bat and started swinging. The injury returned, a dull ache at first, increasing to a blue-hot jolt of pain with each batting practice stroke.

"I think we did the right thing by waiting," he said. "I don't second-guess that at all. You've got to wait and see what happens before you go in and do something drastic."

Finally, unable to tolerate the pain, Treadway underwent surgery on his hand in Louisville, Kentucky, and the prognosis was that he wouldn't return before the All-Star break. In performing the operation, hand specialist Dr. Harold

Kleinert took a piece of bone from Treadway's hip and fused it into the second carpo-metacarpal joint of his right hand. He informed Treadway that if the surgery had not been done, a tendon near the affected joint might eventually have ruptured.

"If that had happened, I would have had serious trouble," Treadway said.

Treadway's loss was a major blow because the more the Braves saw of Lyons, the less they liked him. Cox felt he was not a good defensive second baseman, although he had been a starter for the Chicago White Sox in 1989. Privately, Lyons blamed third base coach Jimy Williams for his troubles; Williams, who also serves as the team's infield instructor, saw Lyons backhand several ground balls in an early exhibition game and told him to get in front of the ball. Lyons tried, made two errors, and the staff dismissed him as a defensive risk.

"He's just not an infielder," Cox would say later. "He can play the outfield fine, but he's not a second baseman."

Lyons had played every position since he arrived in the majors in 1985, including making a pair of pitching appearances. He played everywhere but catcher in 1991 and was charged with only three errors, one at second and two at third.

"I'll be the first to admit I'm not a very good player, but I do have over five hundred hits in the majors," he said. "Somebody told me last year that seventy-eight percent of the players who play in the big leagues never make it to five hundred hits, so I must be doing something right."

Lyons felt increasingly certain he had made a mistake in accepting a $600,000 contract from the Braves. He started wondering to himself whether it would have been better to re-sign with the Boston Red Sox and stay in the American League, where he had played his entire career, rather than try to find a place for himself on a new team in an unfamiliar league. Normally an outgoing personality, a player nick-named "Psycho" for his antics on and off the field, Lyons was uncomfortable with the Braves and his fun-loving nature never emerged.

Convinced Lyons was overmatched as an infielder, Cox would only use him in the outfield, which was already crowded with Gant, Justice, Nixon, and Deion Sanders. Unhappy with his lack of playing time, Lyons considered meeting with Cox and asking for an explanation, but he knew that if he did, the situation could worsen and he could be buried on the bench or worse, released.

"I haven't shown them too much and now they're scared to put me out there," he said. "But you can't prove you can play when you're sitting on the bench."

Meanwhile, Jeff Blauser felt that Treadway's loss might become his gain. Although he's a natural shortstop, the Braves have moved him around the infield since he arrived in the majors in 1987, playing him at every infield position except first base. Like Treadway, he's been labeled a mediocre defensive player, but he has good power and holds a career .262 batting average. His versatility is a blessing and a curse; in baseball, once a player is labeled, it's almost impossible to shake the tag, and Blauser has been labeled a utility player, someone who can fill in at several positions but can't play every day. He hates the tag.

"It upsets me," he said. "It's just like a pitcher who's wild when he was young. He's always going to be called wild, no matter what he does. You can't change people's minds. I was sixth on the team in plate appearances last year, but the Braves say I'm not an everyday player. You figure it out."

Blauser sees himself stuck in a no-man's-land between a regular role and a utility man's job. He played more than the team's twenty-fifth man in 1991, but less than a regular. Given a chance to play regularly, he feels he could be as productive as Pittsburgh Pirates shortstop Jay Bell, a solid offensive shortstop who hit .270 with 16 home runs last season. Even as he collected more at-bats than most regular players, Blauser remained frustrated. He fears the tag of utility player will follow him throughout his career, limiting the number of opportunities he receives to play daily.

Cox likes to platoon players, a position-sharing system that usually benefits the team but angers individuals. Blauser and Lemke share second, Sid Bream and Brian Hunter split time at first base, and Nixon and Sanders share center field. Players feel platooning hampers them because they never play more than two or three consecutive games and don't get a chance to settle in and feel comfortable.

Since Blauser's defense is only average, Cox uses him when the club needs an offensive boost. It's an approach that upsets him because he will frequently be swinging a hot bat when Cox shifts back to a defensive lineup and he returns to the bench. Blauser often wonders if he would be better off traded to another team. The New York Yankees showed some interest several years ago, but they were unwilling to part with center fielder Roberto Kelly and the deal fell through. Since then, regular shortstops Rafael Ramirez and Andres Thomas have departed Atlanta, and still Blauser isn't a regular, playing more at second base than at his natural position.

"I've never believed that being traded to get a change of scenery meant anything," he said. "But I do now. I think a change in scenery is what I need."

As spring training continued and the monotonous routine of morning stretching exercises, batting practice, and afternoon games plodded onward, more problems developed. Reliever Juan Berenguer was unhappy that Schuerholz refused to discuss a contract extension, while Justice created national headlines by commenting on racism in baseball.

Berenguer is 37, a veteran with the plump physique of a weekend softball player. He grew up in Panama and his English is heavily laced with an accent, prompting his teammates to nickname him "Chico." Given an opportunity to become a closer for the first time in his career last season, he responded with 17 saves in 18 chances before disaster struck: He went down with a forearm injury in August and didn't return, then underwent surgery and a bone graft to repair the damage in December.

How did Berenguer suffer the injury? At first he indicated it happened at home while he was playing with his children. Then a story circulated through the clubhouse that a fight between him and pitcher Marvin Freeman during a flight to the West Coast had caused the injury. Much later, Berenguer indicated he had suffered the injury while throwing a pitch to Giants slugger Kevin Mitchell in San Francisco's Candlestick Park.

Wary about how Berenguer would rebound from his injury, Schuerholz told him he'd talk to him about a contract extension later in the season. Actually, he had no plans to open talks at all. Berenguer was being paid $1.2 million in the second year of a two-year deal worth $2.1 million, and Schuerholz figured to let him go after the season.

While Berenguer sat and steamed, Justice popped off and caused an uproar. He is often approached by reporters because he is considered quotable, but occasionally he sticks his foot in his mouth. This time, on a still March morning in the Braves clubhouse, he addressed racism in baseball by asking, "How many white players do you see get abused in the paper? We see it happen all the time with black players. No matter what you do you're still a nigger. Baseball is just an extension of life. When you're on the field, they love you. I can't tell you how many times people have looked at me when I'm off the field and because I wear a nice watch and wear good clothes they think I'm a drug dealer."

Justice was talking quietly and Gant, seated nearby, was nodding.

"Damn right," he said.

Justice was just getting warmed up. He told a story about walking across a parking lot to his car and watching a white woman seated in a nearby car roll up her window and lock her door as he approached. Glancing around a half-filled clubhouse, he added quietly, "There are a lot of good guys on this team, but there are a few who I know use the 'N' word when I'm not around."

He was asked whether replacing Dale Murphy in right field

two seasons ago has worked against him. Is he expected to take Murphy's place as Atlanta's most beloved sports figure? He shook his head.

"There's no way in hell I'm ever going to be Dale-Murphy-perfect," Justice said. "If you're a normal human being, you know you're not perfect. I know expectations are high for me. Fans expect me to do well. If I play baseball well, I'll be all right. If you start slipping, that's when you don't have friends anymore."

When Justice's comments appeared in the paper the next morning, a firestorm of reaction enveloped him. He was blitzed by reporters and camera crews and asked repeatedly to explain himself. Privately, many of Justice's black teammates agreed with him, but he was left to stand alone and defend himself. At first, he beat a hasty retreat, claiming his comments were taken out of context. The next day he relented and acknowledged the quotations were accurate.

"The only thing I wish I hadn't said," he conceded, "is about my teammates using the 'N' word. I don't want to cause dissension here."

Life for Justice would never be the same again—not in Atlanta, anyway. The negative publicity generated from his contract negotiations, his refusal to pose during Photo Day, and his comments on racism turned off even the staunchest of his supporters.

"Right now, no matter what I do, it's news," Justice admitted. "Usually the person who is the lightning rod is the guy who tells how he feels. That's me. I'll always tell you how I feel, right or wrong. I won't be in the middle. I can live with myself being that type of person. For as long as I play with the Braves, I'm going to be the one who gets the most flak. I could hit thirty homers and drive in a hundred runs and it won't be enough. I'll be just like Darryl Strawberry was in New York."

As the Braves broke camp, Keith Mitchell wanted to cry. The young outfielder was sent to the minor leagues as the Braves trimmed their roster to 25, and his face betrayed his emotions: He looked like a little boy who had just been told his dog had died. His eyes were misty, his lip quivered, and his voice shook.

"I just don't know what to think," he said. "I don't want to go down there and start all over again."

The final cuts of spring always troubled Cox. He hated calling in players and looking them in the eye as he told them they were being sent to the minor leagues or had been released.

"It's the worst part of my job," he said later. "You're taking away someone's dream."

The end of the road didn't catch veteran catcher Mike Heath by surprise. For weeks he'd been expecting to be called into Cox's office and told he was through. With two capable catchers on hand—Greg Olson and Damon Berryhill—he knew he had little chance of making the club. Heath sat in the clubhouse all morning, awaiting word on trade talks with two other teams, but when the discussions failed to produce a deal the Braves released him. The timing of the move, coming six days before the season opened, upset him.

"That kind of put me in a bind when they waited so long," he said. "This really discourages someone from picking me up."

While Mitchell, Mark Wohlers, and Heath packed their belongings, a smile lit the face of catcher Jerry Willard. He was a long shot to make the club, but injuries eliminated his competition and Cox decided to keep him. Willard, a pudgy, moon-faced man, has been playing pro ball for 12 years, but has played only one full season in the majors. There's not much to like about him in the eyes of most scouts; he's slow and he can't catch or throw well enough to claim a position, but he's a left-handed hitter, which has been enough to keep him on the fringes of the big leagues for five different organizations.

"Average arm, average defense, but a good bat" is how Cox described him. "A survivor."

Willard became a hero in the 1991 World Series when he drove home the winning run with a sacrifice fly in Game Four. Now, in March of 1992, Willard couldn't believe his good fortune in making one more major league club.

"It was a big relief," he said later. "I really wasn't in the picture at the beginning of the spring, but I put myself in the picture with what I did. I was a long shot, but I think I deserved to make the team."

Lonnie Smith was another old-timer who didn't figure to see Opening Day. A veteran of four World Series with four different teams, he was a Cox favorite because of his toughness and durability. Looking around a clubhouse crowded with young outfielders during the first week of spring training, Smith was sure he would be released before the end of March. Now 36, he had a reputation as a horrible defensive outfielder and his speed had steadily declined because of painfully sore knees, yet he was set to begin his fifteenth major league season.

Smith spent the winter wondering if he should retire. His wife, Dorothy, was expecting their first child in September, and he was fearful of what another season would do to his knees. In addition, he wasn't looking forward to replaying his baserunning gaffe in Game Seven of the World Series again and again for reporters, a mistake he had compounded by refusing to talk with the media following the game. Starting off first base on a delayed steal with Pendleton at the plate and no outs in the eighth inning, he had lost sight of the ball when Pendleton drove it toward the left center field wall. He stopped at second base, unaware of third base coach Jimy Williams's frantic waves and shouts. By the time he spotted the ball again, bouncing off the wall, it was too late. Williams was forced to stop him at third, where he remained as Gant bounced out and Bream grounded into a double play. Two innings later, the Twins scored the game's only run and claimed the world championship, leaving Braves fans to moan over Smith's blunder and wonder why he stopped running.

Smith wouldn't talk about it. He had spoken briefly with a

Philadelphia columnist, an old friend from his days with the Phillies, after the game, but refused to leave a back room in the clubhouse to speak with other reporters. He had remained mum on the subject of his gaffe over the winter, though he was vilified by writers throughout the country and had emerged as one of the greatest goats in Series play. Finally, one March morning in a half-empty clubhouse, Smith agreed to discuss the play and revealed the cause of his mistake.

"I made the mistake of not looking in," Smith said. "I heard the crack of the bat and I saw Knoblauch [Chuck, the Twins second baseman] make a fake. Then I saw Gladden [Dan, Twins left fielder] move, and by the time I got to second I had to slow up to see if Gladden or Kirby Puckett would catch the ball."

Pendleton was standing near Smith's locker, listening to his description of the play. He interrupted and said, "I think I was the only one who could see the ball wasn't going to be caught. Lonnie couldn't see that from where he was."

Smith nodded and continued. "By the time I saw they weren't going to catch it and started running toward third, Jimy Williams was holding me up."

After the team returned home, he watched replays of the play again and again, listening as CBS announcers Tim McCarver and Jack Buck offered explanations for his mistake. He accepted the blame, but denied that Knoblauch's fake caused him to slow down.

"By the time I picked up the ball it was just about to hit the fence," Smith said. "The biggest mistake I made was not to look in. I was gambling on Terry not hitting the ball. That was a bad gamble."

Lost in the uproar and conveniently forgotten by most observers was the fact that the Braves still had runners on second and third and no outs. The blame for their failure to score a run that inning belonged to Gant and Bream as much as to Smith, yet only Smith was labeled a goat. Long afterward Smith would look back on the play and remark, "There always has to be a goat in the World Series and it was decided that I would be the one last year. There was nothing I could do about it."

He contemplated retirement. He searched his heart for a reason to stay in the game. He had three World Series rings, a career batting average of .291, and though he would never be elected to the Hall of Fame, he certainly would be remembered as a fine player. So why continue to play? His knees ached and he knew his role with the team would be as a pinch hitter, which he didn't feel comfortable doing. He had always played regularly, needed three or four at-bats a game to get into a rhythm at the plate, and the thought of hitting only three or four times a week didn't appeal to him.

"It's a question of, can I still play or not?" he said. "I know I can, but it's a matter of whether I can take the pain. I still have the desire, but you have to ask yourself whether it's worth it to put up with the pain."

In the end, the decision was simple. Smith was on the last year of a contract that would pay him $1.75 million, and with little chance of finding work next year, even with a pair of expansion teams joining the league, he couldn't afford to pass up the money.

The team was finally set. Twenty-five players, six coaches, and a manager. Two other players—Treadway and Tommy Gregg —would open the season on the disabled list. As they boarded a plane in Little Rock, Arkansas, where they had played their final exhibition game against the St. Louis Cardinals, the Braves were like jockeys preparing for the Kentucky Derby, eager for the race to get started yet apprehensive about what lay ahead.

They had not played like champions during the spring. Cox was worried about the offense, which had been flat and unproductive. He was concerned about Justice's back, which was flaring up again, just as it had last summer. And he was not convinced that Lemke was ready to be a regular.

These thoughts and more tumbled through his mind as the

plane headed toward Houston, where the Braves would open the season in the forbidding Astrodome.

"Are we ready?" Cox asked himself. "Can we repeat?"

The plane droned on and Cox stared out the window, contemplating the long season ahead.

# APRIL

There are worse places to open a baseball season than the Astrodome, but no team is based in Death Valley or on Alcatraz. The Dome is dark and forbidding, its outfield fences are miles away from home plate, and more than one infielder has taken his eye off a popup, lost it among the latticework of supports and the grim background of the roof, and seen it bounce behind him. The Astrodome is the scourge of baseball purists, who envision a major league of grass fields and open-air parks, and can't abide the game being played indoors on artificial turf. Cox counts himself among the game's traditionalists and thinks the Dome should be torn down and a shopping mall erected in its place. He hates it for any number of reasons, but primarily because his teams almost never win in Houston. Last year was an exception: For the first time since 1985, the Braves posted a winning record inside the Dome, though the memory of losing all nine games in Houston two years ago still haunted them.

The coaches' room in the visitors' clubhouse at the Astrodome is a cubbyhole, with just enough room for several lockers, chairs, and a small refrigerator stocked with sodas and fruit drinks. Cox likes to arrive at the park early, usually ahead of even the stadium workers, and sit with one or two coaches, swapping stories. This is one of his favorite times, the prelude to battle, and he delights in listening to Ned Yost's hunting tales or Pat Corrales's stories of being Johnny Bench's backup in Cincinnati.

But Opening Day was different. Cox, who always feels some butterflies before the start of a game, was more jittery than usual. He sat in his tiny office down the hallway from the coaches' room thinking about his lineup and wondering where the team was headed. The offense was a worry. Pendleton and Gant are notoriously slow starters, Justice's lower back was bothering him, and Nixon was to miss the first 18 days of the season as he completed his 60-day drug suspension. Cox stared at the ceiling, rubbed his temples, and decided to bench Lemke and start Blauser at second base, hoping his bat would spark the sluggish offense.

Lemke did a double-take when he saw the lineup. Blauser had spent most of the exhibition season playing shortstop and had played second only a few times during the last week when Lemke was out with a sore hamstring. Cox told reporters he was sitting Lemke down because of the injury, but the second baseman wasn't buying it. Lemke, who looks like the neighborhood nerd, the one who was always the last player picked when teams were chosen for a stickball game, was crestfallen.

"My hamstring is fine," he said. "It's been okay for the last couple of days. What's he doing? I don't understand. I've been the second baseman all spring. I was looking forward to making my first Opening Day start. I can't believe it."

The odds on Lemke just reaching the major leagues were astronomical. He has the rumpled look of a bachelor who never hangs up his clothes, he wears glasses and has the pasty-white complexion of a gym rat. He grew up in Utica, New York, and his high school baseball team often had to wait for the snow to melt before they could open their season. Yet here he was in his fifth season with the Braves, one of the club's best defensive infielders and its top offensive player in the World Series. In the days leading up to the team's arrival in Houston, Lemke often felt chills tingle along his spine as he envisioned being called from the dugout Opening Day and introduced to the Astrodome crowd as the Braves starting second baseman. Now, he thought sadly, he would never get that opportunity.

"I've worked hard for this," he said. "I thought I was the second baseman and now this. Why won't he give me a chance?"

Across the room, Blauser was just as surprised as Lemke. He's a natural shortstop and feels uncomfortable at second base, particularly since he had had so little playing time there this spring. Blauser understood Cox's desire to spur the offense, but he wondered if the offense he added would be negated by his limited defensive skills at second. There were no other surprises in the lineup; Sanders would lead off and play center, Pendleton would bat second, Gant and Justice followed, Bream hit fifth, Blauser sixth, then Olson, Belliard, and Glavine.

For Glavine, it was the first opportunity to demonstrate that last year's 20-win season was no fluke. He was looking forward to silencing his critics, who delighted in pointing out he had been no more than a mediocre pitcher during the second half of last season with an 8–7 record. Glavine is a proud New Englander, having grown up in Billerica, Massachusetts, just outside Boston, and it irritates him that he spent more time defending his winning of the Cy Young Award as the league's best pitcher last winter than he did enjoying the acclaim.

"Everybody thinks I can't do it again," he said grimly. "Well, I'm going to prove them wrong and then I'm going to laugh at them."

At one time Glavine figured hockey was his ticket into pro sports. A standout center in high school, he was drafted by the NHL's Los Angeles Kings and by the Braves a few days apart in June of 1984, but chose to take the $90,000 bonus Atlanta offered to stick with baseball. Still, hockey is never far from his mind. He had accepted an invitation to skate with the Boston Bruins during a practice at Boston Garden last winter, which made Schuerholz cringe when he found out, and figures to be a regular at the Omni later in the year when the minor league Knights open their first season in Atlanta. Although choosing baseball over hockey is a decision Glavine has never regretted, even when he suffered through a 17-loss season with the last-place Braves in 1988, he often wonders if he could have made it in the NHL and is fond of joking that center Wayne Gretsky would have had to change positions if he'd signed with the Kings.

There has been nothing meteoric about Glavine's rise to a place among the game's best pitchers. He served his apprenticeship shackled to baseball's worst team for three years and used the time to study the league's hitters and develop a changeup. A slender left-hander, Glavine has the freckled face and lopsided grin of Huck Finn but the heart of a felon. He is cold and calculating on the mound, warm and gregarious off it. Many pitchers prefer to spend the hours before a start in silent anticipation, reviewing hitters and strategy before they trek to the hill. Not Glavine. He'll talk golf, girls, hockey, or any of a dozen other subjects right up until game time. Once he enters the dugout, however, he's all business. And, like so many other players, he follows his superstitions. Just before he heads to the mound in the first inning he pops a piece of Sugarless Bazooka gum into his mouth and slips an extra into his back pocket. That's all he will chew throughout the game. In 1991, during a game against the Giants, Glavine was sitting in the dugout waiting to pitch the eighth inning when the gum fell out of his mouth. Aghast at upsetting his routine and fearful the spell was broken, he quickly rescued the gum from the dugout floor, washed it off and popped it back into his mouth. Then he went out and pitched a scoreless inning.

Before a game Glavine dresses in the same T-shirt he wore in his previous start, he sits in the same spot in the dugout throughout the game, and he hangs his jacket on the same hook. He takes the same number of warmup pitches every inning and refuses to vary his routine: two fastballs, two sliders, two curves, one changeup, and another fastball. Before he leaves the dugout he takes his cap off and puts it back on three times. He does that again following his warmup pitches.

Glavine insists he isn't superstitious, but he keeps several rabbits' feet hanging inside his locker, a gift from a fan several years ago. He can't bring himself to get rid of them.

"I figure there has to be something left in them and they're not going anywhere now," he says. "But I'm not superstitious."

Opening Night in the Astrodome didn't hold the same magic for the Braves that it would have if they had opened elsewhere. Only 25,000 fans showed up to greet the Astros, who had finished a distant sixth last season and didn't figure to improve their standing this year, and the lack of excitement settled on the field with a visible pall. Glavine didn't care; he gave up a pair of early singles, then roared through the Astros, holding them hitless after the second inning as the Braves won 2–0.

Twenty-four hours later it was John Smoltz's turn. He gave up three more hits and one more run than Glavine, but hung on for a 3–1 win and a rare sweep of the Astros in the Dome. The brief road trip complete, the Braves boarded their charter flight to Atlanta, eagerly anticipating sleeping in their own beds for the first time in seven weeks, anxious to greet the raucous crowd at their home opener the next day.

Returning home is always sweet, but this occasion raised goosebumps on everyone's skin. The Braves hadn't played in Atlanta–Fulton County Stadium since Game Five of the World Series and a sellout crowd was expected to help celebrate the raising of the National League pennant and the presentation of their league championship rings. At 3:00 P.M., four and a half hours before game time, fans were already wandering around outside the stadium holding signs asking for tickets. Music was blaring, lines formed at the concession stands by six, and fans without tickets huddled around smoking barbecue barrels in an outer parking lot, ready to watch on a fuzzy TV hooked to a sputtering generator. For players and fans who had endured the lonely seasons of the middle and late 1980s, the celebration was an eye-opener.

"Our opening nights were nothing like this," marveled former Braves pitcher Rick Camp. "I don't know if we ever had a sellout on opening night."

Blauser, along with Glavine, had been here since 1987. Grinning, he said, "I don't remember any [home openers]. I'm selectively forgetting."

Being a Braves fan is now considered chic. Former president Jimmy Carter and wife, Rosalynn, attended the game, along with Braves owner Ted Turner and his wife, Jane Fonda. Actor Arnold Schwarzenegger and wife, Maria Shriver, joined them in the box next to the home dugout. The welcoming roar of the crowd was beautiful. What followed was ugly: The Braves lost to the Giants 11–4, though no one was particularly disturbed by the defeat. Afterward, still admiring their rings, each with an elaborate diamond-encrusted "A" as its centerpiece, they were transformed into little boys.

"Awesome," Lemke said. "You can't put a value on a ring like this."

Cox, equally impressed, said, "I'm a wedding-band-only guy, but I will wear this one. It is beautiful."

Beautiful though it may be, the ring was a punctuation mark to last year's storybook season. The 1992 story was beginning with a troubled outlook. David Justice's back was giving Cox a headache. Justice had promised to strengthen the area with a winter conditioning program. He took up karate, lifted weights, did stretching exercises, then felt the pain return when he began swinging a bat again. If it had been any other player, no one would have questioned the injury, but Justice's teammates remembered the rumors about his dancing in Atlanta nightclubs during last season's injured spell.

Many players were cool toward him, some barely able to hide their hostility, and none offered sympathy.

Justice knows he is not well-liked, that many of his teammates perceive him as being more concerned about his own statistics than the team. Even his girlfriend, actress Halle Berry, admitted soon after meeting him that she thought he was arrogant after watching a television interview. Perhaps that was why Justice was willing to swing through the pain this year: He wanted to prove to his teammates that he could play with an injury, like the well-liked and highly respected Pendleton, who had played for three months with a cartilage tear in his knee last season.

"I'll be in there until I can't walk," Justice told reporters.

The way Justice was swinging, it might have been better if he sat down for a while. He was cautious and tentative during batting practice, admittedly holding back to save his normal stroke for games. Even then, he wasn't the same player. In the two wins in Houston, Justice was nearly invisible in the cleanup slot, managing only one single in eight at-bats. It was obvious his back was bothering him, but Justice was intent on proving he was no quitter. His new approach didn't last long. When his batting average dropped to .059, he decided the pain was too great. On Sunday morning, April 12, he arrived in the clubhouse, saw his name in the lineup, and told Cox he couldn't play. He was scratched and placed on the disabled list. While many people doubted the seriousness of Justice's injury last year, doctors who performed a test on his back confirmed this one: a stress reaction to a small bone adjacent to his lower back, a condition that usually occurs in teenagers.

"It does explain his pain and why it lasted as long as it did," team orthopedist Dr. Joe Chandler said.

Justice had an I-told-you-so smirk on his face after the test results became known.

"I don't feel any vindication," he said. "I knew all along I was hurt. It's just a shame you're not given the benefit of the doubt."

• • •

Justice's loss left Cox in a quandary. Who would play right field and bat cleanup? His response created a domino effect in the outfield. He shifted Gant from left to center, started Smith in left, then moved Sanders from center to right. The result was a speedy, if hardly Gold Glove outfield. Sanders shrugged at the position change. With Nixon out until April 24, nothing could take away from his enjoyment of playing every day, even while playing out of position. This was an opportunity Sanders had been anxiously awaiting, a chance to demonstrate he wasn't a novelty item, a two-sport windup doll following in Bo Jackson's footsteps.

A brash and demonstrative All-Pro cornerback with the Atlanta Falcons, his approach to baseball was just the opposite. He had purposely toned down his act inside the Braves clubhouse and had become a well-liked and well-respected teammate, a player everyone had hated to lose when he returned to football last August. Still, a bit of his cocky nature emerged as he considered this season.

"This is Prime Time's year," he said. "I'm going to be successful, no matter what it takes."

His lack of success in baseball gnawed at him. Sanders couldn't stand to fail at anything, even fishing. He was an avid fisherman, and his daily competition with Avery and Nixon following spring training games became a running joke in the clubhouse. Each would claim he was the better fisherman and in the end Sanders would walk off shaking his head, bemoaning his lack of an honest partner. His confidence on the baseball field was expressed more quietly: Give me a chance to play every day, Sanders said simply, and I'll show the Braves what kind of baseball player I can be. Blessed with extraordinary raw talent—he was perhaps the fastest player in the game—Sanders had failed miserably in his previous opportunities. A left-handed hitter, he had a .178 average in two seasons with the New York Yankees, then hit .191 in part-time duty with the Braves in 1991. His experience with the Yankees especially galled him; he was shuttled back and forth between the minor leagues and the Bronx Zoo, rushed into the Yankees lineup with too little experience, then hustled out when he failed. There was a time when the pressure on him to succeed in New York became so great he contemplated taking a knife and purposely cutting himself between his thumb and first finger so he couldn't grip a bat and could return to football full time.

"Four years ago he was absolutely the worst Triple-A player I'd ever seen," Braves first base coach Pat Corrales said. "He couldn't hit a fastball, he certainly couldn't hit a curve, and he didn't know what he was doing out there."

While Sanders was in New York, there was a celebrated run-in with veteran White Sox catcher Carlton Fisk, a no-nonsense type who berated him one day for failing to run out a popup. Sanders heatedly told him the days of slavery were over and white men didn't control blacks anymore. The two men almost came to blows on the field, and Sanders never forgot the incident. He left New York with a chip on his shoulder, angry and embittered at the Yankees for their treatment of him and determined to prove himself a baseball player. He made substantial strides in improving his overall game. During spring training he worked on his bunting—the threat of which drew infielders toward him and allowed him to slap the ball by them—and he no longer appeared helpless against left-handed pitchers. While the Braves stumbled along early in the season, winning as many games as they lost, Sanders began to take off. By the time the team reached Los Angeles on April 16 to meet the Dodgers for the first time since last September's showdown series, he was leading the league in hitting and had drawn rave reviews from his teammates, as well as from some of the crusty veterans of the game.

"You knew sooner or later Deion was going to break out like this," Gant said. "He is just too good an athlete not to be a real good player in this game."

Hugh Alexander, the elder statesman in baseball's fraternity of scouts, has been around the game for 50 years and has seen its best players. From a seat behind home plate, where he scouted for the Chicago Cubs, he watched Sanders evolve from a curiosity into a legitimate major leaguer. In his eyes, it was almost an overnight transformation, for it usually took players four or five years in the minor leagues and another two or three in the majors to reach the same point. Sanders's progress took his breath away and left him feeling amazed.

"I tell people the really great ballplayers can beat you five different ways: throwing, running, fielding, hitting, and home runs," Alexander said. "Only the great ones can excel in all of those phases. Now, I tell you what. Sanders is not in that group and maybe he never will be, but I'm not sure if I've seen a more exciting player. If he stays in this sport and gives up football, he could be one of the great ones. There's nothing prettier in baseball right now than watching him hit a triple."

The problem was that the Braves had to share Sanders with the Falcons. His divided loyalties had resulted in his missing all of the postseason last year. It was Schuerholz's hope that he could be persuaded to drop football altogether, but Sanders said repeatedly that it would never happen. He enjoyed having two careers and, more important, two paychecks, and the attention of the dueling sports fed his ego. While Schuerholz and Sanders's agent, Eugene Parker, discussed a contract that would keep him a Brave beyond July 31, when he was scheduled to report to the Falcons, the Nike shoe company jumped into the picture and made it even more difficult for Sanders to give up football. Nike planned a new ad campaign with Sanders as its focus and offered him a three-year deal worth a million dollars a year to endorse their products. The only catch was, Sanders had to play both sports or the deal would be worth only $100,000 each year. As the negotiations with Nike continued, representatives of L.A. Gear called and said they wanted Sanders too, and two or three other athletic shoe companies contacted Parker to make a bid for him. Suddenly, Sanders had become one of the hottest properties in sports. Parker was optimistic that his client would soon make more money in endorsements than he did playing the two sports.

Sanders was enjoying himself on the field as Cox penciled him into the lineup every day. While the Braves lost three of four games to the Dodgers in Los Angeles, he went 6-for-17 in the series, with a triple and a double, and the Dodgers grudgingly admitted he was for real.

"I watched him last year and I thought, well, he's trying, but he's no Bo Jackson," Dodgers center fielder Brett Butler said. "This year I'm so much more impressed. He's a throwback player with a modern-day grace and style. You look at Deion and you think of guys who have had great talent, but they're just good players because it was their choice to be mediocre. Not Deion. He's working hard to get to that upper level. If he keeps working hard, the sky's the limit."

From worst to first and back again. The Braves bused down the coast from Los Angeles to San Diego and dropped two of three games to the Padres. Glavine was shelled in the final game, lasting only four innings and allowing 11 hits and 6 runs. It was not a happy group that returned home in last place with a 6–10 record, three and a half games out.

Lonnie Smith underscored the team's frustrations by exploding against home plate umpire Jim Quick after striking out for the third time in the eighth inning of the series finale. He was ejected, then had to be dragged off the field by Corrales, Williams, and Pendleton as he continued a shouting and finger-pointing performance directed at Quick.

However, the trip wasn't a total loss. Soon after they arrived, Cox and Yost hopped a trolley outside the team's hotel and rode it to Tijuana, Mexico, for a shopping expedition. Cox, who owns horses, was on the lookout for some saddles, and he came back a happy man. He found two beautiful leather saddles and, with Yost helping him barter, paid a total of $230 for them. The only problem was getting the saddles

Bill Zack

back to the hotel, then onto the plane. The pair hefted the saddles on their backs and walked back to the trolley.

Recounting the story later, Yost admitted, "We looked like a couple of greenhorns."

Before they left Tijuana, a small Mexican boy approached Cox and asked, "Are you Bobby Cox?"

Flustered, Cox nodded and smiled. The boy, dark-haired and grinning, said, "Boy, you sure do look better in person than you do on TV."

Lifting the saddles again, Cox and Yost walked away laughing.

After being away from home for 59 of 63 days since February 20, the Braves returned to Atlanta to open a nine-game stand against the Astros, Mets, and Cubs. After dining on room-service food and packing and unpacking a half-dozen times in the past weeks, the players were overjoyed at the prospect of a home-cooked meal and the chance to sleep in their own beds.

"I may just go out on my street at six A.M. and yell and scream I'm so happy to be home," Pendleton said.

"I feel like Judy Garland," Olson said. "There's no place like home, there's no place like home."

Since spring training opened in February, the Braves had been home three nights. They opened the season with 16 consecutive games, all but 4 on the road. It was evident that being away for so long had begun to wear on the team. Since leaving Atlanta 12 days ago, they had been flat, and the recent performances of the pitchers and offense concerned Cox. The staff gave up 39 hits and 17 runs to the Padres in three games, with no starter lasting more than four innings. The offense appeared only in spurts, scoring 10 runs one night and 2 the next. But Cox was worried most about the bullpen, because no reliever had been consistent. Alejandro Pena and Mike Stanton lost consecutive games in Los Angeles and none of the six relievers had been sharp for more than an inning or two.

As Cox, wearing a Stetson he dons while he's home, headed into the clubhouse in the early afternoon of April 24, he had something to look forward to: Nixon had been reinstated by the commissioner's office and was eligible to play, and Cox planned to start him and Sanders together for the first time. Although he knew the combination would remain intact for only a few days, because as soon as Justice was ready he would return to right field, he was still eager to see what impact two of the game's fastest players could have hitting one-two in the lineup.

In one sense, the results did not disappoint him. In three games against the Astros, Nixon and Sanders reached base 10 times. But with the offense continuing to sputter, they scored just one run.

Smith and Nixon are close friends, lockers next to each other in the Braves clubhouse, and have similar life experiences, both having undergone drug rehabilitation. However, Nixon's return sent Smith back to the bench and he was unhappy. He wanted his agent, Dick Moss, to discuss his release or a trade with Schuerholz—a man he despised—to get him out of Atlanta as soon as possible.

"I'd like to play a couple more years and that's not going to happen here," Smith said. "I'm not going to be happy just hanging around and taking up space."

Smith and Schuerholz's relationship goes back several years to when both were in Kansas City, Schuerholz as the general manager and Smith as a .287-hitting outfielder. Following the 1986 season Smith opted for free agency, but the owners' collusion meant he received no offers and was forced to accept Schuerholz's offer of a minor league contract. He blames Schuerholz for the subsequent downward turn of his career, which hit bottom in 1988 when the only major league team that would give him a chance was the Braves. Cox, then the Braves general manager, signed him to a Triple-A contract and promised him an opportunity to return to the majors; a year later Smith was named the National League's Comeback Player of the Year after a .315, 21-homer, 79-RBI season, and Schuerholz was left with egg on his face.

Ever since then, Smith has hated the general manager, whom he privately calls "The Little General," and he was horrified to see Schuerholz named Braves general manager. If not for injuries and his big contract, Smith, now 36, probably wouldn't still be with the team. Nixon's drug suspension worked in Smith's favor; if Nixon had not been suspended last September, Smith would not have had the opportunity to reach the minimum number of plate appearances he needed to guarantee the final year of his contract. Without that guarantee of $1.75 million this season, the Braves would have bought out his contract and cut him loose last winter. And if outfielder Tommy Gregg had not suffered a broken hand in spring training, Smith probably would have gotten his wish to be traded or released late in spring training. Smith is probably best suited to playing in the American League as a designated hitter, but Cox loves his fearlessness and considers him a good hitter, and he is well liked by his teammates. He was a steadying influence on the younger players and had been named the judge of the club's kangaroo court, a job that always goes to a respected veteran. So he stayed, though his unhappiness threatened to disrupt the team.

"The longer I stay, the more frustrated and disappointed I become, and I don't want to spoil what they have here," Smith said. "I figure it's difficult to come out here every day and not cop an attitude. I don't want to be a distraction to them and myself. It's best I leave before I no longer can deal with it."

Smith grew up in the Los Angeles area, and he was bitterly disappointed at making only two brief appearances in the four-game series at Dodger Stadium. He had family and friends watching and was embarrassed at meeting them after every game and having to explain why he didn't play. On the trip home, he reached a decision: He would go public with his complaints and hope the threat of his disrupting the team would force Schuerholz to trade or release him. His unhappiness was wearing on everyone. The veterans like Pendleton and Bream knew what he was going through and sympathized, but the younger players like Justice and Hunter could only see his anger and blamed Schuerholz for not making a trade.

Cox's own response to unhappy players was to ignore them. Rarely would he call any player into his office to discuss his lack of playing time. He left it up to the veterans to handle internal squabbles and to keep the younger players in line. Although Schuerholz was willing to dump Smith, Cox didn't want to let him go. He liked having veterans on the bench and thought Smith would become more valuable as the season wore on. Though Cox was aware of his unhappiness, he figured Smith's loyalty to him would eventually win out. It had been Cox who had rescued him from baseball's scrap heap in 1988, and he counted on that memory to appease Smith now.

As April drew to a close, the Braves won five straight games in Atlanta, beating the Astros twice and sweeping a three-game series from the Cubs. Four of the victories were by shutout. Their record stood at 11–11, which left them tied for fourth place, only one game behind the three division leaders, the Reds, Padres, and Giants. Despite the win streak, things weren't rosy inside the Braves clubhouse. Reliever Kent Mercker was sitting in the bullpen wondering why he was in Cox's doghouse, and Steve Lyons was holding his breath, uncertain of his immediate future. He drove into the tunnel beneath Atlanta–Fulton County Stadium and parked in front of the Braves clubhouse on the afternoon of April 27, knowing it would probably be the last time he did so. With Justice ready to come off the disabled list, Lyons figured he'd be cut to make room on the roster. With Sanders playing well, Cox and Schuerholz met and decided Lyons should go, though the Braves would have to eat his $600,000 salary. Schuerholz still defended signing him last winter, saying, "It wasn't a mistake. It was the proper thing to do at the time. Who knew how well Deion was going to play? We had a clear need for a guy like Lyons."

What surprised the Braves was discovering that Lyons was

no infielder and that his bat was even weaker than their scouting reports indicated. Though he wasn't surprised by the move, Lyons felt he never got a fair shot with the team and indicated he would declare himself a free agent rather than accept a demotion to the minor leagues.

"They're cutting their losses," he said. "I'll look for another job. I'd consider going back to any team that shows an interest and will give me a chance to do what I can for them."

During the next two months, Lyons kept popping up on the transactions list in *USA Today*. He signed with Montreal, then was released. He returned to Boston and shortly thereafter was demoted to Triple-A Pawtucket.

With Lyons gone, one Brave breathed a sigh of relief, while another cursed the decision. Hunter, hitting .081, was sure he would be sent down to the minors to make room for Justice. "I thought it would be me because I have an option left," he said. "I thought they'd keep the veterans." Meanwhile, Smith had been hopeful the Braves would use the opportunity to release him, and when he learned Lyons was gone instead he was bitterly disappointed.

But Smith was no more unhappy than Mercker, who was rarely being asked to warm up and only occasionally appeared in games. He was upset by his lack of work and found it ironic that while other teams were constantly pursuing him in trade, his own manager refused to use him.

A first-round draft pick of the Braves in 1986, Mercker likes to kid that his name has been tossed around in trade talks so much he keeps a packed suitcase by his front door. Yet in the back of his mind he knows the club is unlikely to trade him because he is that most valuable of pitchers: left-handed, able to work as a starter and a reliever, and the owner of a 90-mph fastball. He sealed his fate in a Braves uniform when he worked six innings of the first combined no-hitter in league history last September, dominating the Padres along with Wohlers and Pena. That was the kind of performance the Braves had been expecting from him since he made his major league debut in 1989, and they weren't about to give up on him and deal him to another team.

Despite the club's high hopes for Mercker and his great promise, Cox was still wary of using him when the game was on the line. Truth to tell, Mercker was a manager's nightmare. Cox was never quite sure what he would see when he brought the left-hander into a game, though he was fairly certain he would be left breathless and his heart would be in his throat by the time Mercker retired the side. Cox had rarely witnessed a one-two-three inning from Mercker. Usually a walk preceded an out, a full count was worked to every other hitter, and two or three pitches bounced to the backstop. So he began calling him into the occasional game where a lead was safe, or the rare blowout, hopeful that Mercker would use the opportunity to polish his control.

Though Mercker knew the criticism was warranted, he felt if he worked more, his command of the strike zone would improve. He was stuck in a catch-22 and was left to ponder his future in the small bullpen tucked into the stands along the right field line.

"I don't feel like I'm part of the team," he said. "I don't want us to lose, but the only time I get in a game is when we're losing. I don't know what's better, to hope we lose so I can get some innings, or hope we win even though I won't pitch at all. That's terrible. I shouldn't feel that way."

By the end of the month, the starting pitching had begun to carry the team. Facing the Cubs in Atlanta on April 29, Smoltz strode from the mound after pitching the seventh inning and was greeted by thunderous applause. Puzzled by the reception, he glanced about and saw the announcement on the center field scoreboard.

"The Braves have just set an Atlanta record with 31 consecutive shutout innings," the message read.

Smiling hugely, Smoltz stepped lightly into the dugout and considered a record that had endured for 29 years, since the Milwaukee Braves days of Warren Spahn and Tony Cloninger.

"That's quite an accomplishment," he said later.

The pitching staff, which posted seven shutouts in 1991, had six shutouts already, including three straight and four in the last five games. The three straight shutouts tied the franchise record, held by the 1959 and 1963 Milwaukee clubs.

Braves pitchers had allowed two runs in their last 45 innings (0.40 ERA) and were within hailing distance of the major league record for consecutive scoreless innings, a mark of 56 innings held by the 1903 Pittsburgh Pirates.

"It's a pretty good feeling sitting in the dugout watching them pitch," Cox said.

Pitching coach Leo Mazzone, a rotund and balding man, just watched with a bemused smile.

"I'm just kind of laying low and letting these guys go," he said.

The offense was also beginning to show signs of life, with 22 hits and 14 runs in the three-game sweep of the Cubs. Catcher Damon Berryhill, making his first start against his former teammates, unloaded his third homer in the eighth inning of the 8–0 finale, a three-run drive that carried over the right field wall. Nixon, replacing Sanders at the top of the lineup, stole a base and scored twice, while Pendleton extended his hitting streak to 10 games and lifted his batting average to .306.

"We started a little slow, but now we're getting great pitching and a decent amount of hitting," Berryhill said.

However, while everyone's bats shook off the April chill, Justice remained cold. He returned to the lineup in the same funk in which he had left, still trying to find his stroke. His average was down to .048 and he looked uncomfortable and confused at the plate. The good news, he pointed out, was that he was swinging without feeling any pain in his lower back.

"It's like spring training all over again," he said. "My timing feels a little off, but that's to be expected. I'll feel comfortable with more at-bats."

# MAY

The Los Angeles riots that followed the acquittals in the Rodney King case hit home with several players. Pendleton, Hunter, and Smith grew up in the Los Angeles area, and Pendleton in particular was worried about family and friends still living in the violence-scarred neighborhoods. He watched clips on television of the rioting in the south central area of the city and could still identify the streets, buildings, and playgrounds of his youth, though his family moved north to Oxnard when he was nine. Pendleton knew the horrors of a city under siege. When he was five he scrambled behind an ice-cream truck as the first gunfire of what would become the Watts riots opened around him. For weeks afterward, as he and his sister walked to school they saw a National Guardsman standing on every street corner.

Pendleton was worried about his grandmother, whose home was in the midst of the rioting. She was trying to sell the place, he said, then shook his head ruefully at the absurdity of his remark.

"Yeah right, like she's gonna be able to sell it now," he said.

A plump little man with a round, earnest face, Pendleton was everyone's big brother and confidant. He earned the admiration of his teammates by playing the final three months last season on a battered and painfully sore left knee, as gritty a performance as anyone could recall having seen for many years. He had the solemn air of a church deacon and played the game like an executive at a power lunch, plotting strategy and sizing up his opponent's weaknesses in a single glance. Pendleton was all business on field, and no other player, not even Bream or Smith, commanded the respect he did. Cox described him as the team's unofficial captain and called on him regularly to help iron out problems. During the stretch drive last September, when Hunter and Mitchell cracked up their cars in alcohol-related accidents one night, it was Pendleton who ushered them into a small room off the clubhouse the next day and talked quietly with them. As Hunter related the one-sided conversation later, Pendleton spoke like a firm parent.

"Sid [Bream] is into making speeches. Terry isn't," he recalled. "Terry likes to lead by what he does. He wants you to follow him onto the field. He just told us what a mistake we had made and that we had to be a little more cautious."

Baseball writers who vote on the various postseason awards are notorious for giving little weight to anything other than a player's statistics. Nonetheless, Pendleton was their choice as the league's Most Valuable Player in 1991, even though Pittsburgh's Barry Bonds had more home runs and RBIs. The writers recognized that the Braves would not have won the division without Pendleton's contributions on the field and his leadership in the clubhouse. Though he played down the award—"It will mean more to me after I retire"—he was immensely proud of the achievement and liked to jab Reds manager Lou Piniella by asking innocently when was the last time an MVP failed to make the All-Star team. Piniella had slighted him last year, selecting several of his own players to be All-Stars instead of Pendleton, and it irritated him. Despite a pair of Gold Gloves and several outstanding seasons, Pendleton had never been an All-Star, and he made no secret of his desire to play in the midsummer classic.

As Pendleton and the Braves continued watching on television, the flames of the Los Angeles riots fanned and spread across the country. A series at Dodger Stadium was canceled, games at San Francisco's Candlestick Park were rescheduled, and still the violence continued. Atlanta was not spared. Angry crowds milled about the downtown area, not far from Atlanta–Fulton County Stadium, and a bomb threat was telephoned to the Braves offices May 1, several hours before the start of a night game against the Mets. The lack of security at the stadium was a running joke among the players, but Stan Kasten didn't inform Glavine, the team's player representative, of the threat. The call was investigated quietly and determined to be a hoax.

"Everyone who needed to know about it was informed immediately," Kasten said. "It was determined to be a crank call. Any threat was cleared up well before the game began."

The next day, in the wake of more violence in the downtown area and an 11:00 P.M. curfew, Kasten and Schuerholz huddled and briefly considered canceling the second game against the Mets. Mayor Maynard Jackson was pressing them to consider the idea, going so far as to express "reservations" during a televised news conference about playing the game. But Kasten and Schuerholz were adamant about going ahead, and there were no disruptions as Glavine beat Dwight Gooden 3–0.

Though Justice had returned to the lineup and his back was not bothering him, he continued to search for his stroke. He is a very impatient hitter and is just as likely to change stances following an 0-for-4 performance as to listen to hitting coach Clarence Jones's advice to stick with one stance and give it a chance to work. When he's not hitting well, Justice wants to know why and he starts to tinker with everything. He backs away from the plate in one game and if he doesn't get a hit, he'll edge closer the next time. He'll stand as erect as a statue one day, and if that doesn't work he'll crouch the next day. His constant shifting from one stance to another aggravates Jones, who wants him close to the plate so he can use his quickness to drive inside pitches, but Justice is stubborn and insists on doing things his way.

As a result of his offensive troubles, he was hearing boos and catcalls from home fans for the first time. He reacted by pretending it didn't bother him. The jeering followed him from the batter's box to the dugout, then out to right field, a stream of abuse that grew louder as his slump deepened. Justice, who could do no wrong in the eyes of Braves fans in his first two years, had fallen from grace and might never regain his throne.

"It's not like I didn't think one day it would happen," he said. "Everybody struggles at one time or another. I expected the boos. I won't call it unfair because they paid to see a good performance and they're not seeing it."

But the boos bothered him more than he let on. Inwardly, he seethed at the abuse he received from people he calls "fair-weather fans," and he stopped signing autographs before games. Justice had always been gracious with his signature, though he limited it to kids and would ignore any adult asking him to sign a card or ball. He made a ritual of moving along the right field stands after batting practice to sign autographs, but now he headed directly to the dugout and disappeared into the tunnel without a glance back.

"Those same people who are asking me for my autograph will be booing me during the game," he said. "I'm not signing for them."

Signing autographs is a pleasure and a pain for players. On one hand they're happy for the attention, but it is also grueling labor attempting to satisfy the thousands of clamoring fans who thrust pennants, bats, balls, cards, and hats at them for signatures. Many players have become jaded about autographs because they feel most fans are asking solely to increase the worth of their card collections. When he does sign, Justice often fights back by personalizing his autographs, which eliminates the collectors' value. Other players refuse to sign more than two or three cards per fan. Still others won't sign bats, because they feel those will soon be auctioned off to the highest bidder.

"When I was a kid everybody just did it for the fun of it," Glavine says. "Now, it's changed immensely. If ten guys come up to you for an autograph, maybe two are there for the fun of it."

"When I played they wanted you to sign one thing," Cox says. "Now they give you six to ten items to sign. There was no money in it back then. Now it's a business and it's all adult collectors. You never had an adult ask you for an autograph before. Now I'll bet over fifty percent of the people asking for autographs are over twenty-five years old."

There is a story passed along by a security guard at the Braves spring training complex in West Palm Beach that two years ago a creative fan arrived at the park every day with a wheelchair in the trunk of his car. The fan, who was not handicapped, would wheel himself in, park near the dugout and, drawing on the players' sympathies, collect dozens of autographs.

"I guess it just goes to show that everybody is trying to get ahead," Glavine remarked.


Greg Olson didn't want anyone to know how much his left knee was hurting him. It was the same knee that underwent arthroscopic surgery last winter, but after spending seven and a half years toiling in the minor leagues waiting for a chance at the majors, he was fearful of being replaced if he went on the disabled list. He really didn't have anything to worry about because Cox admires his defense and the pitchers enjoy working with him, but Olson was unconvinced. He thought he'd be on the next plane back to the minors if he missed too much time, a thought that made him shudder.

Panned by scouts as a good-field, no-hit prospect, he bounced around the minors, from the Mets organization to the Twins and finally to the Braves, a player labeled as a career minor leaguer. He was nearly ready to retire and become a high school coach when Braves backup catcher Phil Lombardi abruptly called it quits just before the 1990 season opened, and Olson was recalled from Triple-A Richmond to replace him. Three months later, the 29-year-old rookie was named to the All-Star team, and a year later he played in a World Series.

Looking back, Olson admitted, "I think 1990 would have been my last year in the minors. My wife was pregnant and if we had gone through one more year making twenty-five thousand dollars I'm sure I would have had to try and find a permanent job."

Now, making $350,000 and needing another season in the majors to gain salary arbitration rights, Olson was willing to do anything to stay. So, he went quietly into the trainers room where the team's orthopedist, Dr. Joe Chandler, inserted a long needle into his kneecap to drain away the expected fluid buildup. However, there was no fluid there. Chandler moved the needle around, looking for a pocket of fluid behind or below the kneecap, but he couldn't find anything. Olson was turning white as the doctor continued to probe the area, enduring what he later called "the worst pain I've ever felt." Finally, Chandler pumped cortisone into the knee and withdrew the needle, and Olson staggered from the room.

He wouldn't play for three days and when he did, he had to change his catching stance to relieve the strain on his knee, but he was still in the majors and that was all that mattered to him. There had been plenty of days when he squatted behind home plate in a half-filled minor league park and figured he'd never see the inside of a major league clubhouse, so each day here was something special. He delighted in the star status of a major leaguer and was constantly being ribbed by his teammates for pursuing every opportunity to make money and accepting everything offered by the steady stream of sporting goods representatives who visited the clubhouse, so long as it was free. His schedule was a whirlwind of card show appearances, clinics, and other engagements, but he figured he was making up for lost time.

"It took me longer to get here than everyone else," he explained, "so I gotta get it while I can."

Braves pitchers were on a roll, having tossed five shutouts in the last seven games, and Mazzone kept his fingers crossed as their success continued. A dumpy man with the strut of a bantam rooster and the temperament to match, Mazzone didn't feel secure in his job. He knew his tenure was tied directly to the pitching staff's success and if someone started to struggle, he started to worry. At the beginning of each game he'd take a seat on the bench and, except when making his occasional visits to the mound, he'd stay in one spot, nervously rocking back and forth as the game unfolded.

Mazzone was excited about the upcoming road trip to Chicago, Pittsburgh, and St. Louis. He had not seen his wife and two sons since leaving his Rawlings, Maryland, home to go to spring training, and he was anxiously looking forward to a reunion in Pittsburgh.

"It will be a very emotional moment," he said.

Rather than pulling his sons out of school every year and enrolling them in a school in Atlanta or wherever he was coaching, Mazzone felt it best to keep them in their regular school, then bring them south when school let out for the summer. It was a migration his family had followed each year as predictably as the swallows returning to Capistrano.

"My wife and I have been doing it for twenty-one years," he said. "That's the part people don't realize about being in the big leagues. You've got to be very lucky to find the right woman."

There was no one, not even Olson, who appreciated being in the major leagues as much as Mazzone. He had ridden minor league buses from Amarillo to Tucson for nine years, finally retiring after the 1975 season without ever reaching the major leagues. He had once tried to pass for a Mexican while playing south of the border, using the alias Leonardo David Massoni.

"When I got there, they asked me to pass for Mexican so

they could import another American player," Mazzone re-called. "They were only allowed so many. They said I looked Mexican. I asked them, 'Can you do this?' And they said, 'Sure, we do it all the time.'"

When he was finally caught and banished from the league, Mazzone returned to the States and came within a stone's throw of the big leagues. He signed with Triple-A Birmingham, the Oakland A's top farm team, but that's as far as he got. His career fizzled and he accepted a job as manager of the Corpus Christi team of the Lone Star League two years later.

"We won the first two years, and I thought I was really something," he said. "Then the league folded."

Mazzone was devoted to three things: his family, his pitchers, and the Notre Dame football team. During football season everyone knew the best way to draw a rise from Mazzone was to parade past his locker wearing a "Notre Dame Sucks" T-shirt.

"It's just a little knife to Leo, a little dig," Bullpen coach Ned Yost explained happily.

Mazzone could hardly wait to get to Pittsburgh. After months of maintaining a relationship by phone, his family planned to drive from northern Maryland and meet him at the team's hotel.

"The tough part is seeing everyone leave when it's time to go back," he said.

The road trip began well in Chicago with a 6–1 win by Smoltz, but disaster struck two nights later. At Pittsburgh's Three Rivers Stadium, Lemke and Justice allowed a game-ending popup to drop between them in shallow right field in the thirteenth inning, and the Pirates won the game in 16 innings. In the dugout following the play Lemke approached Justice, who turned and stalked away.

"I just wanted to say let's forget it and win the game," Lemke said later. "He didn't want to talk about it."

Although Lemke accepted responsibility for the play, several players said it was Justice's ball to catch, and another pointed out that Justice had made a habit of shying away from those plays, which forces infielders to venture far into the outfield to attempt difficult catches. Before the clubhouse doors opened to the media, Cox blamed Lemke for the mistake, but the next day he told reporters "either one could have caught the ball easily."

Lemke shouldered the blame, though he was furious at Justice for refusing to accept partial responsibility.

"I didn't call for it," Justice insisted. "Until the right fielder calls the second baseman off, it's his ball. Since he was camped under it, I was going to let him have it for the third out. The reason I didn't call for it was because it got real noisy out there and I didn't want to have happen what happened in the Metrodome during the World Series, when we ran into each other."

Nothing was going right. Three days later in St. Louis, Smoltz took a no-hitter and a 9–0 lead into the fourth inning, then was pummeled for 11 hits and 7 runs over the next 3⅔ innings and the Braves lost 12–11. In a clubhouse as quiet as a pharaoh's tomb, Blauser stared into his locker and said softly, "It's a little disheartening to be on the other end of this because we did it to a lot of clubs last year."

There was no excuse for Smoltz's lack of concentration on the mound. He had entered the game intent on extending his shutout streak, 18 innings at the start of the game, and when he yielded a run with two outs in the fourth inning, he lost his focus. He repeatedly cursed the pitch that Cards left fielder Brian Jordan, Sanders's teammate in the Atlanta Falcons' secondary, had sent into right center field for a two-run triple and berated himself for failing to retire the rookie and end the inning. By the time he departed in the seventh, his pitches had become batting practice for the Cardinals, and he strode from the clubhouse without speaking to reporters. The next day, after a sleepless night in which he replayed the game over and over in his mind, Smoltz was subdued and embarrassed.

"A pitcher kills for that many runs," he said. "I went back

to doing some things I shouldn't have and I learned a valuable lesson. For a flash you saw the old John Smoltz and you won't see that very many times."

Most scouts acknowledge that Smoltz has the best stuff of any pitcher on the Braves staff. At the same time, they also agree he falls into the category of pitchers with million-dollar arms and 10-cent heads. Despite his overpowering array of pitches, Smoltz has never been a consistent winner, and more than a few people inside the Braves organization wonder if he lacks the guts to be a dominant pitcher. Glavine doesn't have Smoltz's 90-mph fastball or his knee-buckling curve, but he more than makes up for it with guile and cold-blooded ruthlessness when he stands on the mound. Smoltz has none of that.

Working with sports psychologist Jack Llewellyn, Smoltz has toughened his mental approach, but there are times when he loses his concentration and becomes flustered. Llewellyn, a former college player and coach, has a mop of curly gray hair, an easy grin, and a plug of tobacco in his cheek. At Schuerholz's urging, he and Smoltz met following the pitcher's disastrous first half last year and developed a close relationship. Llewellyn, who is booked around the country as a motivational speaker, helped renew Smoltz's confidence with a short video highlighting his best games and taught him several mental exercises to use while he was pitching. Though the psychologist was initially viewed with suspicion by many players, Smoltz was quickly sold on him, and his transformation from a weak-kneed pitcher into a consistent winner helped the team accept Llewellyn. Watching Smoltz win 12 of 14 decisions during the second half also convinced Schuerholz, so he signed the psychologist to an exclusive contract last winter to work with players throughout the organization.

However, despite his success following the 1991 All-Star break, Smoltz still has a lot to prove. Every now and then the Braves will catch a glimpse of the old Smoltz and the specter is ghastly. WTBS broadcaster Don Sutton, who won 324 games during a 23-year career in the majors, feels Llewellyn is partially to blame for Smoltz's immaturity. He thinks Smoltz is using the psychologist as a security blanket, ready to run to him when anything goes wrong, rather than dealing with his problems on his own.

"I love John like a brother," Sutton says, "but he has to grow up."

While everyone else's attention was focused on Smoltz, Cox was more worried about Alejandro Pena, who took a loss in Chicago after giving up a tenth-inning run, then blew a save opportunity in the 16-inning game in Pittsburgh when the Pirates' Cecil Espy delivered a two-out, game-tying single in the bottom of the ninth. According to radar guns tracking the reliever's pitches from behind home plate, his fastball had lost about five miles an hour, a significant decrease in velocity for a power pitcher. It was a puzzle for Mazzone, the pitching coach who frets about his pitchers the way Father Flanagan worried over his Boys Town flock. He looked at Pena and couldn't see anything wrong, yet the JUGS gun said his pitches were traveling at 85 mph and hitters were pounding him.

In St. Louis, disaster struck Pena again. Called into a game the Braves were winning 5–3 in the eighth inning, he gave up five hits and three runs and the Cardinals took a 6–5 win. The clubhouse door was closed for five minutes before Pena trudged up the carpeted tunnel from the dugout, his face set in a weary and sorrowful expression. He slumped in front of his locker and slowly shook his head in bewilderment.

"I can't believe this is happening," he said. "I don't know what's wrong, so I don't know how to fix it."

Cox was nearing the end of his patience with the bullpen. The Braves had won just three of eight games on the trip to Chicago, Pittsburgh, and St. Louis, and four of the losses came at the expense of the relievers. Each time another one was called into a game Cox and Mazzone held their breath and covered their faces, like kids at a horror movie.

"I'm picking the right relievers," Cox said, "it's just that they're not getting anybody out."

Before the team left Busch Stadium to return home, Mazzone gathered his pitchers around him and delivered a pep talk.

"Don't get down on yourselves," he told them, "and don't start feeling sorry for yourselves. If you weren't big league pitchers you wouldn't be here. Stay aggressive and things will turn around."

Lois Johnson thought she had the answer to halting the club's tailspin. The wife of broadcaster Ernie Johnson, she sent him to the stadium with two dozen four-leaf clovers and ordered him to distribute them to Cox and the players. Johnson felt a little silly asking everyone to wear a clover in his left shoe, but they had worked in the past and as Cox said, "Heck, I'll wear it anywhere if it will help us win."

This time the clover didn't work. The Braves lost two of three games at home to both the Pirates and Expos and fell five games under .500 and back into fourth place. Justice still wasn't hitting and there was growing sentiment in the clubhouse to bench him and play Nixon and Sanders together in the outfield. The pair were sharing center field, a platoon that angered both, especially with Justice playing so poorly. Nixon was especially upset because he felt he had proved himself last season and deserved to be a regular. He telephoned his agent, Joe Sroba, and suggested he ask the Braves to trade him. Sroba, who had negotiated Nixon's $8.1 million contract last winter, a deal that allowed the outfielder to exercise an option to sign with another team after the 1993 season, attempted to soothe him and suggested he wait a while before demanding a trade.

Nixon wasn't soothed. Though he promised to keep quiet, in private he was furious at Cox for playing him only three or four times a week and said he'd air his complaints if it continued much longer.

"I didn't re-sign with this team to sit on the bench," he said. "This is stupid. If they want to keep doing this then they can go ahead and trade me to somebody who needs a leadoff man."

Justice was also upset, but for a different reason. He continued to be booed at every turn, and a "Trade Justice" banner appeared on an upper-deck railing at Atlanta–Fulton County Stadium, a sentiment much of Atlanta seemed to favor. It all came to a boil on an otherwise pleasant evening against the Cardinals, when fans peppered him with peanuts while he waited in the on-deck circle in the sixth inning. After the Braves' 5–1 win, Justice stomped into the clubhouse and, waiting for reporters and television crews to gather around, he raised his voice and blasted the fans by saying, "It's no fun playing at home, at least not for me. I just shook my head after the peanuts were thrown, I couldn't believe it. It takes the joy out of playing at home."

Justice, who had hired a public relations firm several months earlier to help him shape a more positive image, knew he'd goofed again. While his teammates snickered behind his back, Justice wandered past a reporter and asked quietly, "I stuck my foot in my mouth again, didn't I?" The reaction to Justice was predictable. The boos intensified, and Atlanta disc jockeys Christopher Rude and Radical Bradford of 96 Rock began airing a song sung to the tune of John Lennon's "Imagine":

> Imagine, no Dave Justice,
> It's easy if you try.
> No one to call off Lemke,
> Then drop an easy pop fly.
> Imagine all the peanuts,
> Just lying on the ground.
> Goobers.
>
> Imagine, no more Justice,
> It isn't hard, just try.
> No more "Hey Dave, how 'bout an autograph?"
> "No!"
> Then watchin' my kid cry.

Imagine all the peanuts,
With no one else to pelt.
Yahoo.

You may say I'm a dreamer,
But I'm not the only one.
I hope some day they'll trade him,
And the Braves will score some runs.


Justice was angered by the song and vowed never to do another interview with the station. Still, his problems persisted. He continued to swing poorly and his power all but disappeared. Each strikeout, each popup, brought another cascade of boos. Never a popular teammate, he was now one of the last players to arrive in the clubhouse before games and kept largely to himself. His personal life, however, was far more satisfying. Unbeknownst to most of his teammates, he had struck up a friendship with Halle Berry, a gorgeous, doe-eyed actress who was included on *People* magazine's list of the 50 most beautiful people in the world in its May 4 issue. The pair fell in love.

Actually, Justice thought he was in love before he even met Berry. They had spoken on the phone several times before meeting, and Justice said he knew immediately this was the woman for him. After a Sunday afternoon game in Atlanta, he flew to Washington, D.C., where Berry was on location filming Eddie Murphy's *Boomerang*, and returned just in time to take batting practice before Monday night's game. He was almost glowing when he walked into the clubhouse.

"That's the woman who's going to be my wife," he declared. "Do you believe in love at first sight? That's what happened to us."

Still, Justice wanted to keep the relationship a secret and it would be another two months before Berry let slip that the pair were engaged. In the meantime, they saw each other when their schedules allowed, which usually meant the actress would fly to Atlanta to watch Justice play.

. . .

Justice wasn't the only player with offensive woes. Lemke, whose three triples in the World Series tied a record, couldn't lift his batting average above .200. Given a chance to play regularly at second base with Treadway sidelined, he was feeling pressure to produce or lose his job. Cox was making sounds that he'd shift Blauser to second and bench Lemke if he didn't start hitting, which only increased Lemke's apprehension. Part of his problem at the plate stemmed from his sore right shoulder, which he had injured when he dove and gloved a line drive a week before. Now he was barely able to lift his arm above his head and it was painful when he swung right-handed. Lemke talked with hitting coach Clarence Jones, who advised him to stop fretting about his .190 average and concentrate on getting four solid at-bats each game, but he continued to worry about his future.

"I'm always riding that fine line wondering whether I'm going to stay in the big leagues or not," Lemke admitted.

With the offense struggling, Cox couldn't afford to keep Lemke in the lineup, though he had no plans to return him to the minor leagues. The lower third of the order of Olson, Lemke, and Belliard was stagnant, and Cox hoped Blauser could inject some life into the lineup. But shifting from shortstop to second was the last thing Blauser wanted. Still angry at being tagged a "utility" player, he wanted to remain at shortstop and play regularly, not move around the infield whenever someone wasn't hitting or needed a break.

"I was getting to the point last month where I didn't have to remind myself about playing second, it was coming naturally," he said. "But I haven't played there in three weeks and I don't know what to expect."

Lemke was resigned to losing his job, though he knew it probably wouldn't be for long. Cox had made this change before, and it lasted only until Blauser threw a ball into the stands or misplayed a double-play grounder. Still, it nagged at Lemke that he couldn't hold on to his position.

"Some guys bust out early in their careers and some don't," he said. "I use that philosophy to keep myself under control. You just have to wait your turn and your time."

While customs and immigration at the Canadian border are always a pain, most of the Braves enjoy coming to Montreal, if only to take in the show at Chez Paree, where gorgeous nude women are on parade. This was also a favorite city among the players' wives and girlfriends, so players had to be careful about being seen entering the club. Dressed in a sharp-looking sweater and slacks, Olson once approached the club entrance just as Belliard and his wife appeared on the sidewalk from the opposite direction. Striding past the club, Olson greeted the pair with a smile, waited until they had walked on, then made a U-turn and darted through the entrance.

Shopping is another experience altogether in Montreal. Pitcher Mike Bielecki is always amused when he walks into a store, pulls out his wallet, and plunks down a U.S. $50 bill.

"They always check to see if the bills are counterfeit," he laughs. "I put a fifty down on the counter and they call the manager out from the back and he takes it and X-rays it."

Dealing with the language and the food intimidates some players. Bielecki takes the easy route and eats at Wendy's, where he can point at the pictures, while Smoltz refuses to frequent any restaurant that doesn't offer American-style steaks. None of it bothers Nixon, who spent two-plus seasons playing in Montreal and picked up a smattering of French.

"I never had any problems," he recalled. "I liked it here. I took some French lessons, just enough to get by. They really got a big kick out of my broken French."

On this visit, the Braves had more to worry about than their French. Their nine-game road trip began poorly in Olympic Stadium, a mausoleum of a ballpark where they never play well. Expos right-hander Dennis Martinez beat Glavine in the opener, then Stanton gave up consecutive homers to Larry Walker and Tim Wallach in the eighth inning the next night and the Braves lost 7–6. Smoltz provided the only bright spot, rebounding from his St. Louis experience and offering one of the best performances of his career, a 15-strikeout win in the series finale.

With a hard-biting curve and an explosive fastball working for him, Smoltz equaled Warren Spahn's franchise strikeout record, set in 1960, and collected the most-ever strikeouts against the Expos, surpassing the previous record of 14 held by John Montefusco, Nolan Ryan, and Dwight Gooden.

"I don't think I can pitch better," Smoltz said. "It was a day where I felt like I was invincible from the first pitch I threw until the very last."

Convinced he needed to prove something to himself to wipe away the memory of the blown lead against the Cardinals, Smoltz promised Mazzone before the game he'd work nine innings. By the time he was through, the Expos were shaking their heads in stunned disbelief.

"After you face a guy who pitches like that, you just come straight to your locker, throw your clothes off, take a shower, and go home," Walker said. "There was nothing anybody was going to do, so you just tip your hat to him."

Laughing later, Smoltz admitted he became so engrossed with strikeouts, he started ticking them off on his fingers.

"I found myself counting the strikeouts and going after them," he said. "I was bound and determined that when I was in a position to strike someone out, I was going to put them away."

However, the glow from Smoltz's performance didn't last long. The tumble continued in Philadelphia with two more losses, and the Braves were suddenly seven games below .500 and in last place, trailing the first-place Giants by seven games. The second game against the Phils was particularly nauseating because the Braves could do nothing against veteran pitcher Don Robinson, who is so fat he seems to be wearing a pillow beneath his shirt. Nonetheless, in his first start since being released by the Giants, he held the Braves to one hit in six innings and claimed a 5–2 victory.

Cox was becoming increasingly concerned about the

team's ragged play and after a night of tossing and turning he reached a decision. Making out his lineup the next day, he benched Justice and Gant, inserted Nixon and Sanders at the top of the order, and shifted Pendleton to cleanup, a series of moves that resulted in a 9–3 win. Nixon and Sanders were particularly effective, combining to reach base six times and score three runs, yet Cox returned Justice to the lineup the following day and sat Nixon down. Nixon was stunned when he entered the clubhouse and saw the lineup, but anger quickly replaced his shock, and in bitter tones he said, "I don't know if we're trying to win. I don't know what we're doing anymore. I'm confused right now. You've got to put the guys out there that are producing. If we're not winning I'm not going to sit here and tell you I'm happy. We're in last place and I can't say this is okay anymore. I'm ticked off that I can't be back out there today."

Several other players privately questioned the move and suggested the team would be better off sticking with the Nixon-Sanders tandem at the top of the lineup and benching Justice for the time being.

"It's a funny situation," Sanders said. "That's all I'm going to say."

Cox's decision was hard to understand with Justice hitless in his last 17 at-bats and without an RBI in his last seven games. Meanwhile, Nixon was hitting .374 in 26 games and had 13 stolen bases in 20 attempts. As usual, Cox offered little explanation, except to say, "You've got to play your power guy. You can't get him going while he's on the bench."

Nixon, who had promised Sroba he'd hold his tongue, was again considering asking to be traded. A proud man, he had fought for eight years to become a regular outfielder before the Braves, his fourth major league team, installed him in center field last season. At 33, he could see his career winding down and he felt it might be better to start over again with another team rather than return to the bench.

"I really don't know when to expect to play, I really don't," he said sadly. "It's not a good feeling. I'm a little disappointed

I can't play two games in a row. It's not fair for Deion and me right now. I want to know which direction this thing is going."

The bullpen was in disarray with Pena unable to locate his fastball, Marvin Freeman's shoulder bothering him, and Mike Stanton missing his strikeout pitch. In desperation, Cox turned to Juan Berenguer and named him the closer, a move the plump Panamanian had been eagerly awaiting. He was bitterly disappointed when Pena was named the stopper coming out of spring training, and since then he had been muttering about demanding a trade.

Berenguer was still upset at Schuerholz for refusing to discuss a contract extension, and he knew the only way to guarantee a job beyond this season was to reestablish himself as a dominating closer. No saves, no money: It's that simple. But even while Cox was naming him the closer, the Braves made several moves that affected the bullpen and undercut Berenguer's role. Rookie Ben Rivera was traded to the Phillies for a minor league pitcher, and Mark Wohlers was recalled from Richmond. Then Freeman was placed on the disabled list and Pete Smith was recalled. Cox quickly abandoned his plan to use Berenguer as the closer after hearing Richmond manager Chris Chambliss and pitching coach Bruce Dal Canton rave about Wohlers.

Looking on, Berenguer smoldered when Wohlers was used in the ninth inning of the next three games while he sat and drummed his fingers on the bench.

"I need saves," Berenguer snapped. "If I can't pitch here, then they should let me go somewhere else."

Cox was content to use a hot reliever as his closer, and Wohlers would remain his favorite only until he blew a save. Then another reliever would become the closer-of-the-moment, a system that kept everyone in the bullpen unsure of his role.

While Berenguer became increasingly concerned about his future, three other pitchers were doing all they could to extend their careers. Smoltz, Stanton, and Mercker hired a Philadelphia-based physical therapist named Chris Verna to help them stretch and become more flexible, a program that upset Braves trainers Dave Pursley and Jeff Porter. They don't like unsupervised workouts, but the trio persisted, meeting Verna once a month for a rigorous stretching regime.

"The first couple of times it hurts a lot, just ungodly, excruciating pain," Stanton said. "But I can see a lot of difference in my flexibility and I feel looser when I throw."

During a 45-minute session, Verna, who has worked with several PGA golfers and was recommended to Smoltz by his agent last winter, concentrated on the hips, lower back, and legs. Smoltz swore by him, insisting the program helped him add velocity to his fastball.

"My recovery time between starts is better," he said. "Physically, I feel better."

A born worrier, Smoltz got started with Verna after reading an article in *Sports Illustrated* that suggested he would blow out his arm after pitching so many innings before his twenty-fifth birthday.

"If nothing else, this has taken a load off my mind," Smoltz admitted. "I felt I had some potential problems down the road. Hopefully, this is my ticket to ten years in the major leagues."

The Braves finished the trip to Montreal, Philadelphia, and New York with a 4–4 record. The second month of the season ended appropriately enough on a cold, drizzly day at Shea Stadium. The Mets called off the Sunday afternoon game hours before the scheduled start, leaving the Braves stranded in their clubhouse because their charter hadn't arrived at LaGuardia Airport. It was a fitting finish to a forgettable month that began with the Braves one game out of first place and ended with them trailing the first-place Giants and Padres by five games.

# JUNE

**Wincing with** each step he took on battered knees, Pendleton rounded the bases slowly and thought to himself how much his wife, Cathy, watching from behind home plate, would be enjoying this scene in the bottom of the ninth inning. Moments before, he had swung at a low fastball delivered by Phils reliever Mitch Williams and sent it on an arc over the left field wall, giving the Braves the kind of miracle finish they viewed as ordinary last season. Trailing for much of the game, they had rallied for four runs in the final two innings to take a fifth straight win. For Pendleton, who had played seven years in cavernous Busch Stadium in St. Louis, this bottom-of-the-ninth, game-winning homer was his first, and he was enjoying the moment. The noise from the stands was deafening. Hearing thunderous applause was not new, not after last season when Atlanta seemed to explode nightly with 25 years' worth of pent-up excitement, but it still sent a chill dancing along his spine. The fans' signature tomahawk chop (actually borrowed from Florida State football fans), an eerie, haunting chant, had become synonymous with the team, and the stadium in full cry was overwhelming. As he touched home plate and turned toward the dugout, he glanced over his shoulder and pointed to where he had seen Cathy sitting before the game, with several other players' wives halfway up the section behind the screen. With fans standing and applauding, he couldn't see her, but he knew she'd be smiling and waving. After he finished icing his knees, they'd meet in the tunnel and drive home together.

The drive would be filled with laughter and talk of their two children, two-year-old Stephanie and 10-week-old Terry, Jr., whom Pendleton lovingly calls "the little one." He had arrived almost two months premature during spring training, and for a time the doctors weren't sure he'd survive. Early in Cathy's pregnancy it had been discovered she was carrying twins, but a sonogram revealed only one heartbeat. She carried both until Terry, Jr., was born. For days following his birth, Pendleton arrived in the clubhouse each morning with a worried frown on his face, then would head to the hospital when the day's workout was completed to sit with his wife and son. Each day the baby improved, and within a week he was out of danger and Pendleton, smiling hugely, circled the clubhouse handing out cigars.

"I would say it's the toughest thing I've ever been through, and now it's a big sigh of relief and serious happiness," he said.

He felt the same way now, felt the burden of the first two months of the season begin to lighten as the team sharpened its play and began to win regularly. As he drove toward his home in a north Atlanta subdivision, he smiled as he remembered the solid crunch he felt as he connected with Williams's pitch and the rise in the crowd's voice as the ball climbed into the night sky. He chuckled to himself recalling how often he'd swung a bat in his backyard in Oxnard, envisioning hitting a game-winning homer in the ninth inning, the same dream thousands of kids shared. And here he was, one of the dreamers, heading home in an $80,000 Lexus, drumming his fingers on the steering wheel, a smile on his face, looking forward to reaching the ballpark the next day.

. . .

Heading toward San Diego's warm Pacific breezes and the spectacular harbor hotel where they stay, the Braves felt good about themselves. They had won five of six games against the Phillies and the Mets, and had begun to creep up through the division, though the bullpen seemed determined to cause Cox an ulcer before the All-Star break. Pena was fighting through a case of bronchitis, while Freeman was bothered by tendinitis in his shoulder, leaving Stanton and Wohlers in charge of closing games. The experiment with Berenguer as the closer had ended almost as soon as it began; Cox did not like his attitude and his constant complaints about not pitching enough. He had begun using the reliever in a setup role again and Berenguer became more disgruntled. He picked up his first save on this West Coast swing, but he would have to work two and a third innings against the Dodgers to get it, and it would be the only one he earned for the Braves this season. Even after being credited with the save, Berenguer was unhappy. He shook his head the next day and laughed.

"Do you believe I had to go that long for a save?" he said. "That's a joke. What's Cox doing anyway?"

Pete Smith had been added to the bullpen last month after pitching well at Richmond, but Cox had five other relievers, and Smith sat around for three weeks awaiting a chance. Even as Cox struggled to shape the bullpen and define each reliever's role, he did not use Smith, which infuriated him. As the weeks passed Smith grew increasingly angry, and when Cox called him into the office one day and told him he was being sent back to Richmond, he stormed out of the clubhouse wishing the club would trade him.

"I've already proven myself down there, so what's the sense in going back?" he said. "I don't know what I feel, I'm kind of numb."

Smith had been dogged by injuries and misfortune ever since 1984, when the Phillies made him their number one draft pick. He and Glavine had been schoolboy rivals in Massachusetts, then became friends when Cox, in one of his first trades as general manager, sent Bedrosian and Milt Thompson to Philadelphia in exchange for Smith and catcher Ozzie Virgil in 1985. He had twice undergone shoulder surgery since then, and his career had stalled while Glavine's had rocketed. At one time Smith was considered Glavine's equal, included in the group of pitchers tagged "The Young Guns" and hailed as the foundation of an improving Braves franchise. His shoulder troubles had robbed him of his overpowering fastball and his confidence as he kept bobbing back and forth between the Braves and the minor leagues. He had watched Glavine win the Cy Young and be rewarded with a $2.9 million contract, then reflected on his own struggles and noted that his 19 career wins were one less than Glavine had posted last season alone. It was enough to make Smith cry.

Cox decided Wohlers and Stanton would share the closer role, though the pair always made ninth innings adventuresome, a practice that drains the color from Mazzone's face and leaves him rocking feebly on the bench. On one night in San Diego's Jack Murphy Stadium, Wohlers headed to the mound in the ninth inning with the Braves up 3–2 and immediately walked Jerald Clark. Kurt Stillwell followed by bunting safely and Cox could feel his stomach tightening as he stood and watched. Wohlers got two outs, and with runners on second and third Cox had a difficult decision to make. He could intentionally walk the left-handed-hitting Tony Gwynn and load the bases for the dangerous Gary Sheffield, or take his chances with Gwynn, a four-time batting champion.

Cox signaled Olson: Walk Gwynn and pitch to Sheffield. Standing on the mound watching the burly, muscled Sheffield approach the plate, Wohlers felt his stomach doing somersaults. It was on the same mound the previous August that he had made his major league debut in almost the same circumstances: ninth inning, winning run on base, Tim Teufel at the plate. He had become so nervous he backed off the mound and attempted to retie a shoelace while his fingers shook. With Sheffield glaring at him and waggling his bat high over his head, Wohlers was buoyed by the memory of striking out Teufel and earning his first save. He threw a fastball to Sheffield, who chopped a ground ball to end the game.

"That was a little nerve-racking," the lanky, boyish-faced Wohlers admitted. "Your heart beats a little quicker in those situations."

Such is the life of a reliever. They tread a fine line each day between success and disaster, as Stanton showed several days later in Los Angeles. He sauntered in from the bullpen in the eighth inning and got two outs, then gave up a home run to Dodgers left fielder Kal Daniels as the Braves lost 3–2. The next night, he entered the game in the ninth inning and preserved a 2–1 victory by striking out Daniels and Brett Butler.

Stanton is a Texas native, a stocky left-hander who missed almost an entire season with a shoulder injury two years ago. As has happened to many other pitchers who have suffered arm or shoulder problems, the injury has helped him become a better pitcher. By robbing him of his overpowering fastball, it forced him to develop two other pitches and sharpen his control. Cox likes to use him late in games against left-handed hitters because he has an intimidating delivery, ducking his head behind a high leg kick like a turtle withdrawing into its shell, then exploding toward the plate. Lately, it's been a crap-shoot with him in a game. He's been missing with a lot of pitches, leaving them high and over the heart of the plate, and hitters have been pounding him.

Stanton has the perfect reliever's personality. His solemn brown eyes harden when he enters a game and his easygoing nature is replaced with a killer's ruthlessness, a transformation that begins to take shape in the bullpen as he warms up, then emerges as he strides toward the mound.

"I'm definitely a different person from the clubhouse to the field," he said. "I'm laid back in the clubhouse, but I get pumped up when I'm on the mound. I just want to get in there and get the job done."

The other relievers were amused to read in the next day's

newspaper a statement by Cox describing how he likes to get his pitchers back to the mound quickly after a bad outing. Mercker, who is pitching infrequently, was especially taken with the idea. "Does that mean all my games have been good ones?" he asked.

Stanton's loss at Dodger Stadium was the only defeat on the six-game trip. After a sluggish eight weeks, the Braves were finally rolling, having won 10 of 12 games to pull within 3½ games of the division-leading Reds. The cracks in the bullpen were being smoothed over by dominant performances from Glavine and the other starters, and the offense was coming around. However, Cox's continued platooning at first base and in center field made four players unhappy. Sanders was especially disturbed about sitting on the bench, and he exploded one afternoon after entering the clubhouse and seeing Nixon's name atop the lineup again. He threw his bag into his locker and shouted, "What do I have to do to play here? What do I have to do?"

Cox and most of the players were already on the field, so Sanders's outburst was witnessed by only a few of his teammates, who shrugged and shook their heads. Slumping on a picnic table in front of his locker, he hung his head and said, "Man, I felt for sure I'd be in there today. I just want to get back in my car and go home. This stuff is starting to kill me."

Sanders was hitting .329 and had 16 steals, yet had started just three of the last nine games and had compiled fewer than 200 at-bats.

"I hate people writing in the paper that Otis Nixon and I are platooning, because this is not a platoon," Sanders complained. "I was lucky that I got a chance to play before Otis got back and I made the mistake of playing well."

Part of Sanders's anger stemmed from his fruitless negotiations with the Braves. His agent, Eugene Parker, was making no progress in talks with Schuerholz about a contract extension, and Sanders thought the general manager was stalling, hoping his batting average would slip and he could be signed for less. Money is the main focus of Sanders's life. Joking in the clubhouse with Kasten one day, he warned, "You'd better get me signed now, Stan, because the longer you wait, the more it's gonna cost you." Grabbing a laundry basket, he shoved it toward the balding team president and said, "Here, go fill this up with money, then we'll talk."

Sanders would be paid $600,000 by the Braves to play until the end of July, while the last year of his contract with the Falcons would net him $750,000. His deal with Nike earned him another $1 million and his various other endorsements, his television show and appearances would increase his income to close to $3 million this year. It was not enough. He wanted to become the NFL's first $2-million-a-year defensive back, while joining the Braves' millionaires club, which already numbered 13 players. But Schuerholz wasn't biting. With Nixon as insurance against Sanders's leaving to rejoin the Falcons, he figured he could wait until Parker reduced his demands, leaving Sanders to sit and fume on the bench.

And fume he did. Sanders was an All-Pro in the NFL, a marquee player who had the spotlight on him as soon as he exited the locker room. It was a different world for him in baseball, where only a handful of players were regarded as superstars and he was not among them. Sanders had a difficult time handling the lack of respect. He wanted to be the main attraction, the compelling reason for fans to pay to watch a game. He looked forward to November's expansion draft, when the league's new members, Miami and Denver, would stock their teams. Sanders figured the Braves wouldn't protect him and he planned on informing Denver that if they drafted him he would refuse to play. He wanted to play for the Marlins, just across the state from his Fort Myers home, where he could spend his mornings fishing and his evenings playing ball. More important, Sanders would stand alone in the spotlight.

"I'll be the man in Miami," he said.

Brian Hunter was as incensed as Sanders by his lack of

playing time, but he didn't have the leverage of another sport to threaten the Braves. He smoldered while Bream, who wasn't hitting, made most of the starts at first base. Just 24, Hunter had made it plain to everyone in the clubhouse that he felt he should be the regular first baseman and he blamed Cox for slapping a platoon-only label on him. Hunter's attitude didn't make him a popular teammate; Glavine especially couldn't understand his approach.

"What does he expect?" he said. "He hasn't even played a full season up here yet, and he expects to take Sid's job. Gosh, when I came up the first time I just sat still and kept my mouth shut. Brian has got to put some time in first before he says anything."

There was virtually no communication between Cox and Hunter. Cox saw him as the club's angry young man and had little to say to him, while Hunter had no regard for the manager and was constantly second-guessing his moves. After being lifted for a pinch hitter in one game earlier in the season, Hunter was irate.

"He doesn't know what he's doing," he said. "Everybody says he's such a smart manager, but he doesn't know anything."

Actually, Cox was regarded by other managers and general managers as being among the best strategists in the game. When Schuerholz accepted the job of general manager, Cox had already been signed as the manager and the pair had hit it off immediately. Schuerholz said he considered Cox one of the top managers in the game, and had rewarded him midway through the 1991 season with a two-year contract extension. Still, Cox occasionally raised some eyebrows with his strategy during a game. He seldom ordered a bunt late in a close game and often irritated Hunter and Bream by pulling them when a reliever entered, regardless of the inning. It was a practice that especially irked Hunter, because he made far fewer starts than Bream and he hated to come out of a game after only two or three at-bats.

Cox and Hunter's relationship had deteriorated last season

after Cox made him a starter when Bream went down with a knee injury, then resumed the platoon when the hobbling Bream returned. Hunter played well when he was a regular and finished with 12 homers and 50 RBIs, numbers he felt he could double if he played every day. He regarded Bream with a measure of disdain, the same contempt a rising young heavyweight holds for an aging opponent, and couldn't understand why Cox continued to play him.

"They want singles, not homers," Hunter said.

Like Sanders, he figured his ticket out was through the expansion draft, preferably to Denver, where the altitude would give a boost to his towering drives.

Swinging an imaginary bat one day in the clubhouse, Hunter said, "I'm in Denver and here comes the pitch. BOOM!"

There were several players who thought they might be selected in the expansion draft. Blauser was already planning to buy a cabin in the mountains surrounding Denver, while Lemke and Freeman were simply readying their suitcases. But Hunter was the only player eager to leave.

"I can't wait for the season to end," he said. "All I want to do is get out of here."


Bream was playing regularly, but he was dismayed by his continued lack of production and power. He had hit just two home runs and wasn't driving in many runs, which led several players to question why Cox continued to play him instead of Hunter. A deeply religious man who steered most players into chapel service on Sundays, Bream was at a loss to explain his slump, which had dogged him for a year and begun to sap his confidence. Even when he hit a ball solidly it didn't carry as it once did, and privately he wondered if he would ever regain his former swing.

"I can't explain it. It creates a panic in me," he admitted. "I ask myself why the ball isn't jumping like it did last year. I constantly search for that stroke."

Bream was further dismayed by hitting coach Clarence Jones's lack of interest in him. Jones was a friendly bear of a man, a former star in Japan who was credited with helping Justice and Gant develop into power hitters. Bream didn't have the relationship with Jones that many of the black players had, and he felt he had been left on his own to work out his problems.

"C.J. doesn't seem too interested in working with me," he said. "He has his own guys he works with and he can't be bothered with me."

Bream, who left the Pittsburgh Pirates as a free agent after the 1990 season and instantly regretted his decision, turned to a former coach for guidance. He telephoned Milt May, the Pirates hitting coach, and the pair discussed the mechanics of his swing. It was a call Bream would repeat several times as he attempted to work out of his slump.

"What I did at the beginning of last year is the kind of power that I feel is deep down inside me," he said. "But what was I doing then that I'm not doing now? There are times when the ball seems to jump for me and the next time it doesn't do anything. Ever since the surgery I haven't been able to find Sid Bream again."

Brian Hunter would not disagree with that assessment. It left them both increasingly frustrated.


Their unhappy platoons notwithstanding, the Braves reached mid-June on a hot streak. Preparing for their first important series of the season, a four-game set with the first-place Reds in Atlanta, they were playing their best ball of the season. They had swept a pair of three-game series at home from the Padres and Dodgers, but still trailed Cincinnati by three and a half games. The starting pitchers were sizzling. During a streak in which the Braves had won 16 of 18 games, the starters had allowed three earned runs or more just four times, and Glavine, Smoltz, and Avery had been credited with 11 of the victories.

The first game against the Reds was a disaster. Stanton came on in the tenth inning and gave up a two-run homer to pinch hitter Glenn Braggs and the Reds won 7–5. In the bottom of the tenth, Gant was facing reliever Norm Charlton when a fastball tailed in and struck him on the wrist. He was furious, and after angrily throwing his bat aside, he appeared ready to charge the mound. For a tense moment he glared at the pitcher, then he walked slowly toward first base. The next day, leaning against the batting cage waiting for his turn to hit, Gant was surprised when Charlton approached and draped an arm around his shoulders.

"Are you all right? I wasn't trying to hit you."

Gant smiled and shrugged.

"I'm okay," he said.

"Where did I get you? On the wrist?"

"Yeah, lucky it was on the wrist."

Charlton offered his hand and said, "I'm sorry."

Gant watched him go and said softly, "No one likes to get hit, but that was a classy thing for him to do, come over and apologize."

It was Charlton's turn to be angry later that night when Hunter launched a home run against Reds starter Greg Swindell in the seventh inning to put the Braves ahead. Watching from the Reds bullpen, Charlton became infuriated when Hunter stood at the plate and pumped his fist excitedly, then slowly made his way around the bases. Charlton was still incensed after the game, which the Braves won 3–2 in 10 innings, and he warned Hunter.

"I would hate to be in his shoes," Charlton said. "That was a bomb he hit, but it was not as spectacular as he made it out to be. I'd just hate to be in his shoes."

Hunter knew he was wrong to show up Swindell and the next day he considered approaching him and apologizing. He didn't, but he admitted, "I probably won't do it again against them."

After Stanton's failure against the Reds, Cox's musical-chairs bullpen turned next to Mercker. It was just the confidence boost Mercker's fragile ego needed. After two months of grumbling over his role, he finally had an opportunity to show off. Walking in from the bullpen with two outs in the ninth inning of the second game against the Reds, he felt the crowd's excitement wash across the outfield and envelop him, like clouds encircling a mountaintop, and suddenly he felt invincible. He barely noticed Cox handing him the ball or Olson's murmured words of encouragement. The first hitter he faced was Dave Martinez, a pesky left-handed hitter, and he pumped three strikes past him so quickly Cox barely had time to settle into a seat in the dugout. Three more strikeouts followed the next inning and Mercker, pulling a jacket on his left arm, was glowing.

The next night Cox signaled for him again, this time with the Braves clinging to a 2–1 lead in the eighth inning. The same feeling of invincibility settled over him as he reached the mound and accepted the ball. He faced Darnell Coles and Billy Hatcher with runners on first and second and forced a fly from each to end the threat, then worked a perfect ninth inning for his first save. Much later, after the crowd had thinned in the clubhouse and the television lights had dimmed, a rush of color lingered on Mercker's face and his voice was a little boy's discovering the excitement of Disney World for the first time.

"I love that situation," he said. "To me, that's me. When I pictured me pitching in the big leagues, that's what I pictured. The last out of the game with the crowd on its feet."

The next afternoon Mike Bielecki reached the eighth inning with a 1–0 lead before he faltered. He was the club's fifth starter, and his schedule was affected by off-days and rain-outs, leaving him in the difficult position of having to stay sharp while he accepted long stretches of inactivity. It was a frustrating role, one that required him to maintain his pitches with regular workouts in the bullpen while he made infrequent starts. Bielecki was perfect in the role: Low-key, with a self-effacing sense of humor, he knew his limitations and accepted his job. Standing on the mound with a pair of Reds on base and two out, he watched Mazzone approach and figured he was through for the day. Martinez, who had homered twice against him in a game last year, stood ready at the plate, with the dangerous Barry Larkin to follow.

His face stern and his mustache bristling, Mazzone climbed the mound and glared at Bielecki.

"You ain't coming out of this game," he said.

Stunned, Bielecki stared at him and wondered what he was up to. The bullpen is ready, he thought to himself, Mazzone knows I'm tired, yet he's going to leave me in the game.

"You're staying in and you're getting this guy out."

Mazzone turned and marched away and Bielecki was left staring at catcher Damon Berryhill, who shrugged and returned to his position behind the plate. A moment later Martinez chopped a pitch to Bream at first base and Bielecki walked wearily to the dugout, having made 115 pitches in a performance he would regard later as one of the finest of his career. Finished for the day, he slipped a jacket on and watched Mercker get the last two outs in the ninth, then headed for the tunnel, his spikes clicking on the cement floor.

"You don't want to complain, but it's real easy to feel sorry for yourself when you're the fifth starter," he said, seated in front of his locker. "You think you deserve to start more, but there are other guys ahead of you, so what can you do? Nobody wants to hear about it anyway. I've been pitching long enough now that it doesn't bother me much anymore."

The weekend was a rousing success for the Braves, who left the Reds reeling, their lead reduced to one and a half games. Atlanta's pitching overwhelmed Cincinnati in the four games, allowing only 7 earned runs in 38 innings, a 1.66 ERA.

"I'll tell you what," Reds pitcher Jose Rijo said, shaking his head, "the way they're playing right now you have to play perfect to beat them."

There are female fans, and then there are baseball Annies. The Annies, women who hang around ballparks, hotels, and bars hoping to meet players, can be fanatical in their pursuit. Blauser related one story about a woman who began writing love letters to him last year and became so passionate about hearing from him she sent along a telephone calling card with her number on it. The same woman sent him letters every day during a road trip last year, a flood of mail he never opened. He finally became so tired of it he gathered them all, dumped them into a manila envelope and returned them. A week or so later he received a package in the mail and opening it discovered the woman had sent the letters back, cut up into tiny pieces.

"That's when it gets scary," he said.

Stanton had received seven or eight letters from a woman living in a town outside Atlanta, asking him to please write her and tell her if he was happily married so she could get over him. Avery continued to receive presents from a girl who said she had a special feeling for him. Letters arrived in the Braves clubhouse each day containing photographs or telephone numbers from adoring female fans.

None of it bothered the players, except when it intruded on their personal lives. After a recent game Lemke, one of the few bachelors on the team, was followed home by two women. Knowing he was being tailed, he tried to shake them but couldn't.

"I'm the only guy on the team that can happen to because I'm driving a Bronco," he said. "Everybody else is driving cars that go a hundred miles an hour."

He reached his house and had been inside only a few minutes when the phone rang. It was the operator telling him he had an emergency call. He accepted, only to discover it was one of the women.

"Hey, you can't follow me home like that," he told her.

"I thought you were really nice," the woman responded. "But you're a jerk just like the rest of them."


The strange case of Nick Esasky was a haunting reminder to the Braves that their playing careers could end in a flash. A handsome and personable first baseman, he had arrived in Atlanta as a free agent following a 30-homer, 108-RBI season in 1989 with the Boston Red Sox and signed a three-year deal for $5.6 million. At the time it had seemed an ideal marriage for both sides. Esasky made his winter home in Marietta, just outside Atlanta, and had accepted less money to sign quickly with the Braves than he would have received if he'd waited and encouraged a bidding war. From the team's viewpoint, they had moved decisively to secure a power-hitting first baseman, signaling a change in direction for a floundering franchise. The reaction from fans had been positive and for once, Atlanta's media had applauded the Braves.

However, the following spring Esasky was stricken with a mysterious case of vertigo and played in only nine games before being forced out of the lineup. He had not returned. Since then, he had toured the country and been probed and prodded by dozens of specialists, and no one could determine the exact cause of his dizziness. He had exhausted his emotions in coping with the illness, his initial puzzlement over the symptoms replaced by a growing fear, then by resignation as it lingered. He had continued to come to the park and to work out throughout his ordeal, and he had begun to make progress in learning to cope with the vertigo, playing in several "B" games in spring training with occasional success encouraging him. The Braves had headed north without him, leaving him behind to continue playing in minor league exhibition games. Eventually, he joined the Braves' Triple-A team in Richmond, Virginia, to attempt a comeback. Three weeks into the experiment, he had made sufficient progress to feel he deserved a chance to play in the majors again. This was a view the Braves didn't share. Schuerholz wasn't convinced he was ready, and rather than disrupt the team, he wanted Esasky to continue playing in Richmond. Esasky agreed, on the condition the Braves make a decision by the All-Star break: Either recall him or allow him to become a free agent. Schuerholz agreed.

"I want it all to work out here. It would be nice to get back with the Braves, even if it's only for the rest of this year," Esasky said. "But I also have to think of down the road and what's best for me and my career."

While Esasky's career continued, at least for the moment,

Jerry Willard's world came crashing down around him one afternoon in Cincinnati. He arrived in the visitors' clubhouse at Riverfront Stadium to find Cox waiting for him. Seated on the couch in the manager's office, the veteran catcher was told that Treadway was being activated and would replace him on the roster.

"It was a little rough telling him," said Cox, who hated making such decisions. "I'd love to see him stay."

Willard was devastated. After years of shuttling between the majors and the minor leagues, he had begun to feel settled. Though he knew Treadway was close to returning, he didn't believe he would be the one to go, especially since Cox liked to have three catchers on hand. An even stronger argument in his favor, he believed, was his development into one of the league's best pinch hitters, an important role in the National League where managers may use three or four pinch hitters in a game. However, Cox had decided the only catchers he needed were Olson and Berryhill, and rather than drop a reliever to make room for Treadway, Willard was the one to go. He packed his equipment bag quickly in the nearly deserted clubhouse and departed without a glance back.

"I was hurt, crushed," he said later. "I had no idea it was going to happen to me. It took a while to calm down."

Willard declined to report to the minor leagues and became a free agent. He thought he belonged in the major leagues, but no team offered him a job, and several weeks passed before he realized he would have to return to the minors to reach the majors again. He finally signed a Triple-A contract with Indianapolis, the Expos' top farm team, and he was recalled by Montreal in September.

After months of frustration and uncertainty about his recovery from hand surgery, Treadway was delighted to discover he was as good as new. During a brief rehabilitation assignment with the Double-A Greenville, South Carolina, team, he had 5 hits in 11 at-bats and now felt ready to return and play a big role with the Braves. A regular for much of last season, he didn't feel he should lose his job because of his injury.

"I'd like to play every day and I'd like to play the whole game, that's no secret," he said.

However, Cox had no plans to make any changes. He had returned Lemke to the lineup in May, even though he wasn't hitting, because he didn't feel comfortable with Blauser at second base. Blauser didn't have Lemke's quickness or range, and Cox had wisely decided Lemke's defense was more important than his bat. Cox would fit Treadway in when he could, but in his mind Lemke would remain the regular. Treadway took a seat on the bench and before long he too began to smolder.

The Braves arrived in Cincinnati as baseball's hottest team. Since May 27, they had won 21 of 24 games, a stretch dominated by the starting pitchers. Glavine had won 5 straight decisions and led the league with 11 wins, while Smoltz had peeled off 4 consecutive wins and had 8 in all. However, it was Avery's turn in the rotation in the first game, and nothing went right from the start. Cincinnati loaded the bases with three infield singles in the first inning, Glenn Braggs followed with a grand slam, and the Reds coasted to a 7–4 victory. Since losing three of four in Atlanta last weekend, the Reds had done some soul-searching and they were loose and confident the next afternoon against Charlie Leibrandt, a left-handed pitcher who broke into the majors with the Reds 13 years ago. His assortment of pitches topped out with an 82-mph fastball, and his primary weapon was a deceptive changeup. To be successful, he had to spot his pitches with utmost care and work around the strike zone, throwing fastballs and sliders inside and changeups away. Without his control, Leibrandt was unarmed. The Reds were waiting for him and they patiently dissected him, scoring seven runs in two innings en route to a 12–3 pasting. Things became even worse for the veteran pitcher the next day. He was leaning against the fence in front of the dugout, his cap tipped back, watching an old-timers' game as morning sunshine washed across his face. Suddenly, he shaded his eyes and began to groan.

"Oh, my God," he exclaimed, "I know these guys. I played with Bill Buckner and George Foster and Cesar Cedeno. And I played against Ellis Valentine and Bill Madlock. What are these guys doing in an old-timers' game?"

Leibrandt watched for two innings, then slowly turned away, a small smile tugging at the corners of his mouth.

"It makes me thankful for where I'm at," he said. "It also makes me think that in a couple of years I might be out there."

The Braves were thoroughly frustrated by the end of Sunday's game. Rookie umpire Jeff Kellogg made a critical call against the Braves at third base in the eighth inning, ruling Pendleton never tagged a sliding Chris Sabo, who scored moments later, and the Reds held on for a 6–5 win and a sweep of the series. Cox was still fuming afterward and in a rare display of frustration, he kicked his office door and said, "It's a damn shame. [Kellogg] blew the call."

The clubhouse was unusually quiet, and grim expressions marked each face. For three weeks the Braves had been riding high, and their experience in Cincinnati served as a rude return to reality. They were reeling as they headed to one of their least favorite stadiums, San Francisco's Candlestick Park, trailing the Reds by four games.

"I don't think the Reds won the pennant today, but they're in a heck of a lot better position now than we wanted them to be," Glavine said quietly.

The Braves got a kick out of San Francisco. With the possible exception of New York, there are more strange sights per block there than anywhere else on earth. A couple of years ago Blauser was walking along a downtown street and almost stumbled across a man lying in the middle of the sidewalk. Relating the story, Blauser chuckled and said, "He had his legs crossed and a pillow under his head, and he was screaming at the clouds. Obviously, he was an ex–middle infielder. I'm embarrassed to say I stopped and listened to him for a few minutes."

On another visit, Freeman was approached by a woman

and discovered, horrified, that the "woman" was a man. "He tried to pick me up," Freeman said indignantly. "I don't know why we stay downtown. Everything about it is strange."

The visit quickly turned into another "Twilight Zone" episode, at least for Bielecki. Soon after the bus pulled up in front of the hotel, he dashed across the street to Burger King for a sandwich. As he reached the counter to place his order, a customer at an adjoining register began shouting at an employee and started a fight. By the time the melee had cleared and the man had departed shouting threats, Bielecki was shaking his head and thinking, "Well, just another night in San Francisco."

Moments later the same man returned holding a hand inside his jacket, feigning carrying a gun, and Bielecki began inching toward the door. As he told his teammates later, "It turned out to be a bluff, but it was pretty scary. As soon as he took his hand out of his jacket and started swinging again, I bolted out the door."

As strange as the downtown area is, Candlestick Park is even worse. Playing at the Stick is a unique experience because there isn't another stadium in any sport in which the elements play as big a role in the outcome of games. Treadway remembered starting a game on a bright, warm day, the sky a glorious shade of blue, only to be damp and shaking several innings later.

"It was one of the most beautiful days I've ever seen, but along about the sixth inning the wind started blowing and the fog rolled in across the top of the stadium and the temperature dropped about thirty degrees," he said. "Everybody was out in short sleeves and had a good sweat going and suddenly everyone is shivering."

That's Candlestick. Dale Murphy once attempted to track a fly ball against an azure sky at the Stick, lost it, and had it fall in front of him as a run crossed the plate; the Braves lost the game 1–0. Two years ago pitcher Pete Smith was on the mound when Giants catcher Terry Kennedy sent a screaming line drive up the middle. It struck Smith on the side of his head, just above his ear and rolled into foul ground, and Kennedy trotted into second base with a double. It seemed every time the Braves played at Candlestick something weird happened, and this visit was no different. After the first game of the series was rained out and Smoltz took a 4–3 win the next afternoon, it was Avery's turn in the finale. He was at the plate in the third inning against Giants left-hander Bud Black and sent a towering drive to right center field. Outfielders Darren Lewis and Kevin Bass gave chase, but the ball descended over the fence for a home run, Avery's first in the majors. However, second base umpire Jim Quick lost the ball against the confusing background of wire fence and grandstand and ruled that it had bounced on the sun-baked warning track and hopped over the fence for a double. Cox trotted out and asked Quick to get some help from the other members of his crew, but he refused and his call stood. Two innings later a TBS replay clearly showed the ball going over the fence on the fly.

In the eighth inning Black caught Nixon leaning and picked him off first base. A moment later Pendleton slammed his thirteenth home run. Then Justice launched a monstrous shot toward the second deck of the right field stands, but the wind caught it and blew it foul. The Braves took a 2–1 loss and Avery couldn't leave quickly enough.

"I don't really care for this park," he said, mildly under the circumstances.

A smiling David Justice
exchanges high fives
with Ron Gant.

John Smoltz, anchor of the Braves' postseason rotation.

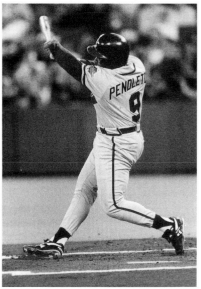

Terry Pendleton's compact swing made him the 1991 MVP; his professionalism and leadership abilities made him the team's unofficial captain.

Second baseman Mark Lemke turns an easy double play.

Jeff Blauser, one of the many players caught in the infield shuffle.

Otis Nixon.

6

7

Brian Hunter, another member of
Bobby Cox's unhappy platoon.

8

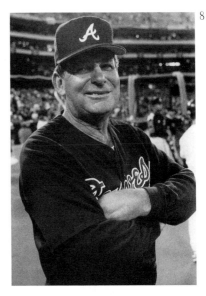

Bobby Cox.

The hint of a smile on Lonnie Smith masks the unhappiness of his season; nonetheless, he was an effective reserve and had one grand moment.

Reliever Kent Mercker, who faced a young Brave's dilemma: untouchable for his potential, unusable down the stretch.

Charlie Leibrandt exults in the embrace of Damon Berryhill after pitching the division-clincher.

12

Steve Avery.

Greg Olson's
season ended
prematurely, but
he still proved a
good-luck charm
in the playoffs.

13

The Braves swarm over the ecstatic body of Sid Bream (white-gloved fist extended at left) in the delirious moments following their Game Seven comeback win.

Francisco Cabrera hoists the National League championship trophy in the Braves locker room. Javier Lopez is on his right, Vinny Castilla behind his left shoulder.

Don Sutton interviews Tom Glavine in
the riotous locker room following
Game Seven of the playoffs.

Ted Turner exults with wife Jane Fonda
at the playoff victory; Rosalyn and Jimmy
are seated with them at far right.

16

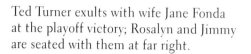

17

John Smoltz missed the tag on
Roberto Alomar at the plate in
World Series Game Two,
but umpire Mike Reilly missed
the call, negating the run.

18

19

Kelly Gruber runs Deion Sanders back to second before tagging him for the "triple play" that wasn't. The flap over umpire Bob Davidson's mistake diverted attention from Devon White's sensational catch that got it all started.

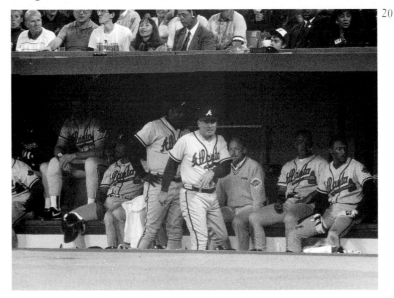

20

Bobby Cox showed his frustration with the helmet toss that led to his Game Three ejection.

# JULY

Bobby Cox sat in his office making out a lineup and wondering when Gant was going to begin hitting again. During the past month his bat had appeared infrequently and he had looked increasingly uncomfortable at the plate. When Gant was going good, his swing was a short, chopping stroke, like a lumberjack's felling a tree. When he struggled, he swung wildly at nearly anything that didn't roll to the plate. His slumps descended on him swiftly, a black cloud that scuttled across the sky and remained fixed over him like an umbrella. Usually, with some extra hitting and a conference or two with Jones, he would emerge a sadder and wiser hitter. But this slump was different. Despite his best efforts he could not shake loose from it and, as if it were quicksand, the more he struggled, the deeper he sank. There was plenty at stake. He had never been named an All-Star, and if he didn't get himself turned around quickly, he wouldn't be named this year either.

The Braves figured Pendleton would be voted by the fans as the All-Star team's starting third baseman, and Cox, as the manager of the league champions, would name the pitchers and the extra players. As Piniella had done the year before, he would like to add three or four of his own players to the squad. Glavine was a sure thing, but Smoltz and Gant were on the bubble. Gant, who liked to play down the significance of being named an All-Star, thought he should have been on the team the past two seasons. After demonstrating his power and speed with consecutive years of more than 30 homers and 30 stolen bases, he could make baseball history with a third straight 30–30 season, yet he had never been an All-Star and it bothered him. He included himself among the game's best sluggers and it annoyed him when he didn't receive the same acclaim as hitters like Darryl Strawberry and Jose Canseco. He had been particularly upset last winter when he felt his 30–30 season went largely unnoticed, so he went to a jeweler and custom-ordered a large gold 30–30 pendant, then slipped it on a chain and wore it around his neck to remind everyone of his achievement. It was the same desire for recognition that led him to a Miami car dealer last spring to purchase a $235,000 Lamborghini, the same car Canseco had parked in his driveway. He loved to show it off and the price sticker remained affixed to one of the car's side windows for weeks as he drove it around West Palm Beach. The day after the car was delivered, Gant took it onto a back road outside the city to see how fast it would go and was awed when he easily reached 150 mph.

But he couldn't buy recognition from fans and writers as easily. He had finished a distant sixth in the MVP voting last season, garnering a solitary third-place vote, and the lack of respect gnawed at him. He believed it was an extension of the attitude writers had displayed after the 1988 season when voting for the league's Rookie of the Year. Despite leading major league rookies in home runs, RBIs, runs, and extra-base hits, he had finished fourth in the balloting, behind Reds third baseman Chris Sabo, Cubs first baseman Mark Grace, and Dodgers pitcher Tim Belcher. He had carried a grudge ever since.

The lack of attention following the World Series galled many of the Braves, particularly the black players, who received few endorsement offers from the Atlanta business community. Pendleton was the first Brave since Dale Murphy to be named the league's MVP, yet he hadn't received a single offer last winter. Gant was taken aback when he was not approached to do any commercials. It was frustrating for the blacks, who saw Olson being asked to pitch everything from water beds to rental cars, and heard Schuerholz doing radio spots, when they had not received the same offers.

That was why Gant thought the All-Star game was important, though he hated to admit it. Like the playoffs and the World Series, the All-Star game was a baseball showcase. He saw it as an opportunity to be recognized on an equal footing with some of the game's superstars and figured some of the attention was bound to spill onto him. However, his slump jeopardized everything. If he failed to be selected for the team with his own manager in charge, it would not only devastate his confidence and cause him to lose a $50,000 bonus from the Braves, but it would provide further proof that he remained far below the game's top players. The more he thought about it, the more he struggled. He arrived at the park each day hoping one good game would snap him out of his funk, then left the clubhouse after midnight angry and confused.

Just as headstrong as Justice at the plate, Gant entered the season intent on changing his approach to hitting after his average fell from .303 in 1990 to .251 in 1991. A dead pull hitter, he began trying to spray the ball to all fields, a plan he eventually recognized was a mistake. He was laying off many pitches he once clobbered, his power disappeared, and he became tentative and undisciplined at the plate. As the All-Star game loomed and his average continued to plummet, Gant panicked.

"I wanted to make the All-Star team so bad I started pressing and then got into some bad habits," he reflected later. "You can't break bad habits that quickly."

Cox hated picking the backup players and pitchers for the team. Inevitably someone got left off the squad who deserved to be on it and the ensuing backbiting and finger pointing was a headache. Cox discussed his picks with National League president Bill White several times, but refused to say who he was considering. With nine wins, Smoltz figured he needed one more to make the team, while Gant was hopeful Cox would overlook his declining average and lack of production over the last month and name him an All-Star. But he had to admit that his struggles weren't making it easy for Cox to do that.

The league had never been able to offer the Braves and Reds a reasonable explanation for why they were placed in the West when divisional play began in 1969, rather than the East with New York, Montreal, Pittsburgh, and Philadelphia. Two teams in the Central Time Zone—St. Louis and Chicago—had been included in the East, and Kasten had complained bitterly about it for years, arguing that it created a competitive disadvantage because the Braves made several extra trips to the West Coast each season. The schedule had become a headache for all teams, but it was especially troubling to the Braves, who traveled 10,000 miles more each season than most teams. Each winter when the schedule was released, most players took one look at it and groaned. Done by computer, it often appeared to have been drawn up by monkeys. Two or three times each season the Braves had to play a series on the East Coast, then fly to the West Coast to play just three games before returning home. Even though they flew on Delta charters, the travel was exhausting. Finally, baseball seemed ready to set the divisions right. It was proposed that the Braves and Reds shift into the East, with St. Louis and Chicago moving to the West. However, the shift required the approval of all four of these teams, and the Cubs refused because they feared they would lose viewers on their WGN superstation. It all came to a head in early July when commissioner Fay Vincent sided with the majority and ordered realignment starting with the 1993 season. Kasten applauded his decision, saying it was long overdue, and many players expressed relief that they would only have to make two trips to the West Coast each season.

"I'd rather take a two-hour plane ride than a four-hour plane ride," Pendleton said.

But the Cubs refused to yield and the Braves' joy was short-lived. A day after Vincent made his decision, Chicago's ownership obtained a court injunction halting the realignment, and ultimately they would succeed in getting the plan scrapped. Greed had triumphed over common sense.

Credit Tim Kominski for putting Tomahawk, Wisconsin, on the map. Little did he realize the uproar he would cause after he dropped off a note at the WTBS booth while taking in a Braves game two months ago.

"Hello, from Tomahawk, Wisconsin," it read.

The note had been passed along to broadcasters Pete Van Wieren and Don Sutton and the fun began.

"You really think there is such a place?" Sutton asked on the air.

"No," Van Wieren replied. "I'm sure there isn't."

Within an hour, WTBS had been flooded with faxes and telegrams—at least 80, by one estimate—saying that yes, indeed, Tomahawk did exist. Van Wieren suggested that Tomahawk would be a perfect "sister city" for WTBS. That sparked an avalanche of correspondence from other would-be sister cities, a deluge of videotapes, T-shirts, banners, and Chamber of Commerce brochures, which didn't slow down for weeks. The broadcast team named Tomahawk its official charter sister city, and named all the other applicants—all 214 of them, including entries from Puerto Rico and quite a few from Canada—sister cities, too. But that wasn't the end of it. Van Wieren and WTBS producer Glenn Diamond accepted an invitation to visit Tomahawk, and the entire town of 3,500 turned out to greet them. While he was there, a man approached Van Wieren, handed him a pair of buffalo head nickels, told him to carry them in his briefcase the rest of the season and the team would return to the World Series.

"I've kept them there ever since," Van Wieren said.

Tomahawk and the Braves proved to be a perfect match. And the town's high school baseball team—the Hatchets, of course—advanced to the state finals for the first time ever soon after Van Wieren's visit.


Trade rumors were buzzing all around the team. Schuerholz was convinced that the source of all such rumors was a New York City bartender, who created them as he served suds to the city's sportswriters, who in turn passed them along to their readers. Eventually, the rumors ended up on ESPN and were reported as coming from reliable sources, which was hilarious because the percentage of truth in each "trade" story was heavily outweighed by the pure nonsense. Still, baseball wouldn't be the national pastime without fans and writers speculating on trades and Schuerholz knew it, though he was often irritated by the constant stream of stories that the players heard and he was expected to respond to. Although the weeks preceding and following the winter meetings each December usually produced the juiciest trade stories, there was no stopping the rumor mill once it got started during the season. Like a Detroit assembly line, writers and broadcasters took fragments of information and produced their own trade rumors, which became more ludicrous with each telling.

Often, a story would take on a life of its own, glimmer like a firefly for a brief moment, then fade away, replaced quickly by another rumor. ESPN's Peter Gammons, a veteran writer who was used by the network to report on baseball news, became a joke in the Braves clubhouse. It began in spring training, when he reported that Brian Hunter and Mark Wohlers were the players to be traded to the Pirates for Barry Bonds. The news had swept the clubhouse like an out-of-control brushfire. Afterward, Schuerholz and Pirates general manager Ted Simmons swore Hunter and Wohlers were never in the deal. Gammons continued to report trade rumors, none of which ever panned out, and before long his name became synonymous with ridiculous stories.

It became a standard greeting to approach a teammate with, "Did you hear what Gammons said last night?" After relating the proposed trade, the two players would walk away laughing and shaking their heads. His latest rumor had Mercker going to St. Louis for reliever Lee Smith, a deal Schuerholz swore he had never discussed with the Cardinals.

"I wish Peter would let me know about the deal I'm going to make because it's the first I've heard of it," he said.

Mercker had become accustomed to hearing his name brought up and had laughed and said, "I lead the league in trade rumors." It was true. Seldom did a week go by without his hearing he was headed elsewhere, which had bothered him when he first came to the majors but now was good for a chuckle. Although most teams in baseball had inquired about Mercker at one time or another, the Braves were not about to part with him. Many left-handed pitchers don't fulfill their potential until their late twenties and Mercker, at age 24, had plenty of time to develop. Still, the rumors of his imminent departure kept coming, marching in like a parade of toy soldiers, only to be cast aside with disdain by the front office. No sooner did the Mercker-for-Smith deal make the rounds than another equally absurd rumor found its way into the clubhouse. This one had Mercker going to Seattle for veteran second baseman Harold Reynolds and first baseman Pete O'Brien, a pair of position players the Braves had no interest in acquiring.

"I think the Braves would have to get Ken Griffey, Jr., and Edgar Martinez, too," Mercker joked.

Schuerholz dismissed all trade rumors, even the ones with grains of truth in them. He was loath to admit he was interested in another team's player and would frequently skirt the truth with any writer who approached him and asked about a potential deal. However, even while he feigned uninterest in a player, he would frequently have his scouts looking him over and filing reports. Schuerholz loved to work quietly behind the scenes to make a trade, then spring it suddenly with an "Oh, by the way" announcement. He had pulled off a pair of trades last summer to strengthen the bullpen, getting reliever Jim Clancy from the Astros and Pena from the Mets, and he wanted to tinker with the bullpen again. Although Cox had returned Pena to the closer role, and Stanton and Wohlers to jobs as setup men, nightmares of Pena's troubles in May still haunted him. Schuerholz kept his fingers crossed that Pena's fastball wouldn't disappear again, but what he really wanted was a dominant closer, like Cincinnati's Rob Dibble or Oakland's Dennis Eckersley.

Soon after he became the Braves general manager, he hired Bill Lajoie, the former GM of the Detroit Tigers, as a special assistant. Lajoie, widely respected in baseball circles as an unerring judge of talent, had worked quietly in the background since joining the organization. He had scouted both leagues, though his focus was mostly on the American, with which he was most familiar, and Schuerholz read his reports with an eye toward making a trade. While the Braves were in Chicago for four games with the Cubs, Lajoie headed to Boston's Fenway Park to watch the Red Sox and see how baseball's all-time save leader, Jeff Reardon, was throwing. He came away thinking Reardon could help the Braves, filed a report, and headed to his next assignment. Schuerholz, of course, denied there was any trade brewing between the Braves and Red Sox.

"It's just another product produced by the rumor mill of baseball," he said.


Chicago's Wrigley Field was a favorite among players, for it evoked memories of an era long past. The ivy-clad outfield walls and hand-operated scoreboard belonged in the 1920s, and the snug grandstands provided an intimate atmosphere not found in many ballparks. The players also liked coming to Wrigley because the Cubs played a lot of afternoon games, leaving them free to prowl Rush Street in the evening.

Blauser loved playing at Wrigley. He liked to describe himself as a throwback to the old-time players who once played there and he thought the old ballpark best captured that image. Once, in one of his rare serious moments, he had sworn he would play the game for free. His claim drew a big laugh because the Braves were paying him nearly a million dollars and he was forced to admit that he had not yet offered the club a refund. Truthfully, Blauser probably would have played the game for nothing. His lighthearted nature hid a deep love of the game, and even after eight years as a pro a part of him still couldn't believe he was being paid to play. Standing in the worn brick dugout at Wrigley, looking across the expanse of thick outfield grass toward the center field bleachers, did something to him. Often he felt he had stepped back in time when he came to Wrigley. In his mind's eye a black-and-white film reel spun and suddenly there was pitcher Charlie Root, dressed in a baggy flannel uniform, on the mound, and Babe Ruth at the plate, gesturing toward those same bleachers. In the next instant Ruth's bat flicked in a blurry swing and the ball climbed into the sky and fell among the crowd in center field and Ruth trotted in a pigeon-toed gait around the bases, all the while motioning at the Cubs dugout.

Blauser would have fit in neatly among the players of Ruth's era. He is a blue-collar type, a player blessed with more determination to succeed than actual physical ability. Playing a position mostly inhabited by nimble, graceful players, he is a plodder, a mule among thoroughbreds. He is a better hitter than a defensive player, and Cox replaces him with Belliard whenever the Braves hold a lead late in games. It is an effective system, though it drives Blauser crazy to take a seat on the bench and watch the ninth inning unfold without him.

He had started just one of the three previous games against the Cubs when he climbed the stairs leading to the visitors' clubhouse on July 12. It was a dreary Sunday morning on the shores of Lake Michigan, blustery and cold, and he reached the clubhouse before most of his teammates and was pleased to see his name in the lineup, though he was hitting seventh, not his favorite spot in the order. The game started an hour late after rain squalls passed through the area, and when Blauser reached the plate in the second inning against Cubs starter Frank Castillo, a right-hander with a hard sinker and slider, wind gusts had reached 23 mph and had torn clumps of ivy off the outfield walls. He settled into the batter's box, his bat held straight up behind his right ear, and when he swung, a powerful, compact stroke, the ball flew on an arc into the left field stands. He came to the plate again the next inning and struck out, then had to wait until the sixth to bat again. Castillo was still on the mound and Blauser launched another of his pitches into the teeth of the wind, dropping it into the right field seats for his second home run of the afternoon.

The game was tied 4–4 when he reached the plate in the eighth and accepted a walk from Cubs reliever Jim Bullinger, and it was still tied in the tenth inning when he faced former Braves pitcher Paul Assenmacher with two men on base. The afternoon had become progressively cooler and the wind couldn't chase away the shadows that covered the infield. Assenmacher, a tall left-hander whose best pitch was a knee-buckling curve, kicked his leg high and delivered the ball over the heart of the plate. The crack of Blauser's bat came an instant ahead of Assenmacher's groan. The ball curled into the left field stands and Blauser rounded the bases with a bit of baseball history tucked under his belt. He became the fourth shortstop in major league history to homer three times in a game. All three of his career multiple-homer games had come at Wrigley.

"I've heard in the past the Cubs want to trade for me, but I don't know if they really want me or they just want to get me out of the lineup," Blauser said, laughing.


After tinkering with his mechanics, Pena rediscovered his fastball. The Braves won five straight games against the Mets and Cubs, and he saved four of them by returning to last season's style of overwhelming hitters with 90-mph pitches. A native of the Dominican Republic, he had pitched in the majors for 10 years, mostly in the role of setup man, which was like serving as Rochester to Jack Benny. The great lines all belong to the star, and in Pena's case, all the ninth innings belonged to the closer. He had never received an opportunity to be a stopper until he joined the Braves, an oversight quickly corrected by a desperate Cox, and down the stretch last season he had been the club's most valuable pitcher. He had been called on in 11 save situations, had converted all of them, and then saved three more games in the playoffs. A free agent, Pena, along with his agent, Adam Katz, figured he would be a hot property during the winter, but their asking price of a multiyear deal for more than $5 million turned off every team. He finally accepted an arbitration offer from Schuerholz and settled on a one-year contract for $2.65 million, a raise of $1.65 million, but was sorely disappointed his work had not garnered more interest. Even so, he was one of the club's highest-paid players and figured to be in line for another big raise if he could duplicate last year's success.

Things went wrong from the start. He had been hampered by bronchitis and strep throat, and when he returned he discovered he had lost his fastball. It was his primary weapon, but instead of exploding past a hitter, it waddled to the plate singing "Fly Me to the Moon," and every hitter who saw it grinned happily and obliged. He had searched videotapes of his delivery and worked with Mazzone to spot the flaw that had slowed the pitch to subway speed before he finally felt comfortable again.

As soon as Pena was ready, Cox reinstated him as the closer. Having a dependable stopper in the bullpen made the whole pitching staff feel better. Without Pena, the relievers' roles had been scrambled and the closer's job had been tossed about like a hot potato. With him, everyone was fitted into a slot and handed a specific assignment, one that suited his talents best. Freeman went back to being a middle reliever, a role he enjoyed because he would pitch two or three innings at one time, though the way the starters were going he didn't often get a chance. Stanton, Wohlers, and Mercker returned to jobs as setup men, working in the seventh and eighth innings, sometimes arriving just to face one or two hitters. Occasionally, Cox used Stanton and Mercker as closers if there were left-handed hitters due in the ninth inning, but he preferred calling on Pena to get the final outs. The starters also felt more at ease with a settled bullpen, knowing if they got to the seventh inning with a lead there was a good chance they would get a win. It was a confident staff that swept four games from the Cubs, pitching two shutouts and allowing five runs in the other two games.

Cox made his All-Star selections, picking Glavine, Smoltz, and Gant to join Pendleton at San Diego's Jack Murphy Stadium, justifying his decision to include Gant by saying he had deserved the honor the past two seasons. Smoltz reached the break with 10 wins, while Glavine led the league with 13 and would make his second straight All-Star game start. Gant, who finished seventh among outfielders in the fan voting, greeted Cox's announcement with a lack of enthusiasm.

"I thought I should have had it a couple of years ago," he said. "I have not gotten that much recognition, but I think this will be a good step. I'm sure it will put me in position to get more votes next year."

Cox's decision to add just two Cincinnati players to the team—infielder/outfielder Bip Roberts and reliever Norm Charlton—did not sit well with the Reds. When pitcher Greg Swindell found out he had been left off the team, he angrily tossed a can of cola and stomped into the trainer's room, mirroring the outrage many players felt.

"Only Bip and Norm? That's it?" Chris Sabo said. "You've got to be kidding me."

Piniella had left Pendleton and Gant off the team in 1991, choosing two of his own players instead, Sabo and right fielder Paul O'Neill, which infuriated Cox and the Braves. Turnabout was fair play, Cox figured. He left Swindell and pitcher

Tim Belcher off the team, though a case could have been made for each to be selected.

The three-day break for the All-Star game was a welcome relief for the Braves. The four-game sweep in Chicago had lifted their spirits and pulled them to within two games of the Reds, who continued to lead the division. Atlanta was in second place, 12 games over .500, a far cry from its position at the halfway point last season, when it trailed Los Angeles by nine and a half games. As the Braves packed to return home, Cox, Glavine, Pendleton, Smoltz, and Gant grabbed their duffels and hustled to O'Hare Airport to hop flights to the West Coast. The Braves would work out in Atlanta on the final day of the break, then fly to Houston, where they would open the second half with four games against the Astros. Cox and the others would join them there, having had little time to recover from their All-Star experience.

Willie Mays gripped a bat and stood with Gant in the Padres clubhouse at Jack Murphy Stadium. He had spotted Gant soon after he arrived and had pulled him aside, the "Say Hey Kid" and one of two players he considered his protégés. Mays had been impressed with Gant after watching him play several years before and had advised his former team, the Giants, to grab him if they could. San Francisco general manager Al Rosen failed to act and Mays shook his head sadly.

"Ron started hitting too quickly," he said. "No way we can get him now."

Gant was thrilled to meet Mays, whom he idolized both for his accomplishments and for helping pave the way for other black players.

"He and Hank Aaron played when it wasn't easy for black players to play," Gant said. "That's why I have a lot of respect for them. Those guys really went through a time when you had a reason to be stressed out. They were tough, mentally and physically."

Mays saw a lot of himself in Gant. Along with Bobby

Bonds, they were the only players in the history of the sport to post consecutive 30–30 seasons, and Mays saw a mirror image of himself as a young man when he looked at Gant. He stood in the clubhouse and swung a bat as Gant watched, his forearm muscles rippling as they once did, and a smile lit his face.

"I watch you play on TV," Mays said. "You're too tense. You've got to relax. When you start pressing, you tense up. The best thing to do is step back, take a deep breath, and relax."

Gant nodded as he watched Mays demonstrate his stroke and for a moment he seemed a little boy, his face a mixture of respect and awe. Later, when Mays had finished and departed, Gant couldn't keep the excitement from his voice.

"Wow!" he exclaimed. "There isn't much to say except that he's awesome."

Pendleton was also feeling like a little boy, but for a different reason. Despite needing the three days off to rest his knees, he was thrilled to be an All-Star and was treating the trip like a big adventure. He would be starting alongside a former teammate and close friend, Cardinals shortstop Ozzie Smith, and the two men and their families skipped baseball's gala celebration at Balboa Park the first night in San Diego to go out to dinner together.

"I would have loved to play with Ozzie in an All-Star game in the same uniform, but it's still going to be like old times," Pendleton said. "We're going to have a good time, even if it's only for a couple of innings."

Pendleton had waited a long time for this occasion and he savored the moment. While he had won a pair of Gold Gloves with the Cardinals and was well respected by players throughout the league, he felt he would never truly be regarded as an outstanding player until he was an All-Star. It had finally happened and though he had never cared much for the spotlight, he admitted he enjoyed the attention this time. A part of him viewed all the hoopla with a sense of disbelief and a little voice inside him occasionally asked what the hell he was doing there, but he laughed away those thoughts and made himself at home. One of the first things he had done was to send a batboy over to the American League clubhouse to get a bat autographed by their players, then he did the same thing in the National League clubhouse. He carefully placed each bat in a plastic container, to be shipped home with all the other All-Star memorabilia he planned to gather.

"I'll tell you, the biggest thing for me here is the thrill of being in the clubhouse with all these guys," he said. "When I leave here with an autographed bat, it will be something special to me down the road. When I'm eighty years old, and I hope to get that far, people can say, 'He's lying, he never played ball,' but I got proof. They can't take that away from me. I'm a little kid with this thing. This is big for me."

Cox wondered if George Bush would remember him. He had met the president at a White House state dinner last winter, an occasion made more memorable when he accidentally spilled wine down the ample bosom of actress Barbara Eden, and he and Bush had exchanged sly glances after the uproar had died down.

"We're on a first-name basis," Cox liked to joke. "George and Bob."

Cox hustled into the clubhouse even earlier than usual on the day of the All-Star game because the Secret Service would be combing the rooms with dogs before Bush's visit and no one would be allowed in for two hours. Cox wanted to get everything organized with his coaches, so he went in at 10:00 A.M., more than seven hours before game time, to get things started before the men in dark glasses arrived to search for bombs. The first order of business was to set his pitching rotation. He hoped the first three pitchers—Glavine, Cubs right-hander Greg Maddux, and Mets right-hander David Cone—would each work two innings. Then he planned to send in Cardinals right-hander Bob Tewksbury, then use Charlton, Lee Smith, and Astros right-hander Doug Jones to close the game. That plan left out Smoltz, whom he was determined to get into the game, but he figured he could squeeze him in before the eighth inning, even if it was just for a hitter or two.

Cox enjoyed making out the lineup. It was a manager's dream come true to have the game's greatest players available to him and he appreciated the opportunity. It was also a bit overwhelming. He had Bonds and Tony Gwynn and Ryne Sandberg as starters and Will Clark, Andy Van Slyke, and Gary Sheffield available as reserves, a staggering array of players for a manager used to penciling in Lemke and Belliard as his seven and eight hitters.

"I knew I'd have butterflies before the game," Cox admitted.

For his part, Glavine was intent on surviving two innings without getting hurt or making many pitches. He had started last July's game in Toronto and pitched two scoreless innings, and he was determined to keep his All-Star record perfect. More important, he had family and friends on hand and he didn't want to be embarrassed by the American Leaguers. He remembered facing Boston's Wade Boggs last year, a player he had admired for many years while growing up near Fenway Park, and feeling flustered as he watched Boggs's familiar mannerisms at the plate. It had all seemed a little crazy and for a few seconds he had wondered what he was doing there, standing in front of 50,000 people facing one of the game's greatest hitters, and he had ended up walking him. As he prepared for his second start, Mazzone approached him in the clubhouse and offered him some notes on the AL hitters, but he decided against using them.

"It's not a real game," Glavine thought to himself. "I'm just out here to have fun."

Soon after Bush, accompanied by Hall of Famer Ted Williams, made the ceremonial first pitch, Glavine strode to the mound and began a nightmarish evening. After he retired leadoff man Roberto Alomar, the next seven hitters reached with singles, and before he struck out Texas pitcher Kevin

Brown to end the inning, the AL had scored four runs. Everything Glavine threw to the plate returned past him and snuck through the infield or fell softly in front of an onrushing outfielder. It was at first aggravating, then downright humiliating. No All-Star pitcher had been treated so roughly since Atlee Hammaker gave up seven runs in 1983.

"They hit a few pitching-wedge shots, kind of broken-bat hits that just fell in," Glavine moaned. "That's more broken-bat hits than I've given up all year. As each hit went by me it got a little bit more frustrating."

Glavine's embarrassment mirrored the National League's. Hoping to win the game as a present for departing league president Bill White, they were humbled by a 13–6 score. Of the four Braves players present, only Pendleton took away a pleasant memory. He had a base hit against Red Sox pitcher Roger Clemens, while Gant was hitless in two at-bats and Smoltz faced one batter—Milwaukee's Paul Molitor—and allowed a hit.


The Braves reassembled in Houston and picked up where they had left off: four more wins, which upped their streak to nine straight, two by shutout, and three more saves for Pena. They were the hottest team in baseball and nothing could go wrong, even when Sanders left a bag containing over $100,000 in jewelry in a taxi after a game. He and Nixon had taken a cab back to the team's hotel, and in the darkness of the car's interior he had left behind a small satchel containing his wallet, a Rolex watch and bracelet, and assorted other diamond-studded jewelry. Unbelievably, he didn't realize it was missing until the next morning, then he panicked.

"I know I've got it insured, but I wanted it back," he said.

Sanders called the cab company, gave the dispatcher a description of the driver, and asked if he recognized the man. Before long the company called back, saying the driver had been located and he had the bag. Sanders was estactic and wondered how much he should tip the driver as a reward.

Nixon pushed him to give the man a $5,000 bonus, but Sanders rejected the idea and tipped him $1,000.

"It's a good thing there's some honest people in the world," he said.

Six games behind the Reds 12 days before, the Braves had closed to within one game and everyone looked forward to a day off in St. Louis. In the minds of most players, coaches, and broadcasters there was only one way to spend an off-day and that was on the golf course. There was some lively competition among the players, particularly the team's two best golfers, Smoltz and Leibrandt. As it turned out, the day's outing was more adventuresome than most.

It all started in the hotel lobby when Van Wieren mistakenly grabbed the golf bag belonging to Jim Guadagno, the team's systems operator. He put it in the trunk of his rental car and didn't notice he had the wrong one until he reached the course. The mistake would not have mattered if Van Wieren had not taken his golf shoes with him. Guadagno's shoes were in his bag and after claiming Van Wieren's bag, he was dismayed to discover he had been left shoeless. He trudged into a pro shop and spent $132 on new shoes, then played a good round using Van Wieren's clubs.

"I don't know if it was the clubs, the shoes, or just great golfing ability," Guadagno said.

Meanwhile, Cox and a dozen players were caught on the course by heavy rain. Before he got drenched, Cox fell over an embankment searching for a ball, then wrenched his shoulder when his hand slipped on his driver and he rammed the face of the club into the ground.

"The club just went B-O-N-G," Cox said ruefully and shook his head. "I just about killed my arm."

Smoltz had parked his cart in a storm drain to wait out the downpour when he heard a roaring noise behind him. Glancing back, he was horrified to see a surge of water rolling toward him, a mini–flash flood that almost swept away the cart.

"It must have been three feet deep," he said. "It almost came up over the bottom of the cart. It wasn't a good feeling watching it come at me."

. . .

With the All-Star break deadline behind him, Nick Esasky reached a decision on his future and bade the Braves farewell. He and Schuerholz had agreed that if the team wasn't ready to recall him from Richmond following the break, he could choose to be released. Schuerholz wanted him to stay at Richmond and continue to work on his hitting, but Esasky felt his career was slipping away and if he didn't return to the major leagues he would be forgotten. At age 32, having played nine games with the Braves, he walked away.

"I hated that I was unable to give anything back to the city," he said. "I would have liked nothing better than to end my career in Atlanta. But the Braves have had to move on without me and now I have to move on. I wanted to give Atlanta a chance, but I had to think about my career."

While Esasky was showing signs of improvement and seemed to be coping with his vertigo, Schuerholz was not convinced it would not resurface and plunge him into another nightmare. More important, he was not prepared to change anything on a team that was playing so well. Though he would not offer Esasky any guarantees, Schuerholz told him that if he remained at Richmond he would likely be recalled when rosters expanded September 1.

"Who in the general manager's chair would be dumb enough to disrupt a team that's playing the way we are?" Schuerholz asked. "The answer is nobody."

Esasky gambled that the progress he had displayed at Richmond would interest another team, though he knew it was a long shot. But with no room for him on the Braves, he felt he had no choice but to attempt to resurrect his career elsewhere.

"Right now, I have no idea if anyone else is interested," he said. "I don't know what the end's going to be, but I want to be able to look at myself and say, 'I've done all I could.' "

So Esasky took his release and returned home and the Braves moved on without him. During the next few weeks he would talk with the Red Sox about returning to Boston, but the two sides never reached an agreement. No other team expressed much interest and Esasky did not play again.

"I did the best I could to convince them that in our opinion the best place for him was in the Braves organization," Schuerholz said. "It would have been a nice story for him to get back to the big leagues with us. He and his agents thought he had a better chance of getting to the major leagues with another club. It was his choice."

Juan Berenguer's incessant whining had irked Cox for months. The portly reliever repeatedly said he should be the closer, though on the occasions he had been used in the ninth inning he had not done the job. Cox knew what Berenguer was up to and ignored him.

"The only reason he wants to be a closer is because he wants a contract for next year," Cox said.

Schuerholz had shopped Berenguer around, but had found no takers. Several months earlier he had called his former team, the Royals, and asked if reliever Mark Davis was available, but he and Kansas City general manager Herk Robinson had been unable to strike a deal. Now, with Cox's annoyance with Berenguer peaking, he telephoned Robinson again and proposed a Berenguer-for-Davis swap. Robinson accepted, and also agreed to foot a portion of Davis's $3.6 million salary. Even with the Royals paying part of the salary, it wasn't an even swap; Berenguer was being paid $1.2 million, while Davis was in the third year of a four-year, $13 million contract, a deal Schuerholz had awarded him as a free agent following the 1989 season. However, Berenguer had become such a negative clubhouse presence that everyone was happy to see him go, regardless of who replaced him. Told he had been traded, Berenguer couldn't pack his belongings and depart the clubhouse at St. Louis's Busch Stadium quickly enough. He threw his T-shirts and spikes into a duffel bag and strode for the door, apparently afraid someone would call him back and tell him it was a mistake.

"I don't care if it's a last-place team or anything," Berenguer said before he left. "I'm glad to get out of here. I didn't care where I went, I just wanted to feel like a part of a team again. It was better for me and for the team to go somewhere else."

Davis felt the same way about Kansas City. His two-year tenure in America's heartland had been disastrous, an experience that had shaken his confidence. Pitching for the Padres three years before he had terrorized National League hitters, a left-hander who collected 44 saves using a deadly curve and lively fastball. He was the toast of San Diego, won the league's Cy Young Award, then bolted for the Royals when Schuerholz made his dizzying offer. He had been a complete bust. Inexplicably, his curveball lost its bite and his impeccable control vanished, and he was getting clobbered regularly. His big contract and former status only made things look and feel worse.

"I honestly couldn't tell you what's gone wrong," he said. "I'd like to come over here and forget about the baseball end of things in Kansas City. There's no blame to be placed on anybody. It's just unfortunate the way things turned out."

A soft-spoken man who seemed genuinely puzzled by the sharp decline of his career, he breathed a huge sigh of relief when he left the Royals and returned to the National League. Troubled by his failures, he looked on the trade as an opportunity to recapture his magic and banish the demons that had tormented him for more than two years.

"I don't really think too much about what's been," he said. "It still creeps into my head, but I try and eliminate it."

With the addition of Davis, the Braves had three left-handers in the bullpen, which would allow Cox to use him cautiously, placing him in no-pressure situations to help boost his confidence. Schuerholz and Cox hoped that by September, when the pennant race heated up, Davis would be ready to contribute.

"It's a good situation for Davis here," Olson said. "He gets a chance to attend the Leo Mazzone School of Pitching. That should help."

Even if it didn't, at least one loudly unhappy voice was gone from the clubhouse.

First place belonged to the Braves. With seven straight wins over the Astros, Cardinals, and Pirates following the All-Star break their win streak stood at 12. They had flown past the Reds and claimed first place, the first time they had led the division since April 10. The winning streak, one shy of the franchise record set by the 1982 team to start the season, was dominated by the pitchers, who had allowed two or fewer runs nine times. Four of the games had gone into extra innings, five had been shutouts. Even the East-leading Pirates were overmatched. They had come to Atlanta for a series billed as a possible playoff preview and Glavine had beaten them in the first game 4–3. Another pitchers' duel unfolded in the second game, Leibrandt matched against left-hander Danny Jackson. Justice had produced the game's only run in the second inning by sending a line drive over the left field wall, his first home run in more than a month, and it had remained the team's only hit through eight innings. As the game wore on, Leibrandt continued to tease the Pirates with his changeup, the same pitch the Twins' Kirby Puckett had belted into the Metrodome seats in the eleventh inning to win Game Six of the 1991 World Series. Leibrandt would long remember that night; Puckett was the only batter Leibrandt faced that night, and he trudged from the mound feeling numb, collapsed into a chair in front of his locker, and sat unmoving, staring at the floor.

"I've never seen a guy sink so low," Cox said.

Leibrandt's despair hid deeper sadness. He had not told anyone that his father-in-law was seriously ill with stomach cancer and after Game Seven he learned he had died. Yet that real tragedy actually helped Leibrandt regain his focus.

"I was more worried about how my wife was doing than one lousy mistake in a baseball game," he remembered. "That made my heartache go away."

The changeup remained Leibrandt's primary weapon and when he exercised precise control it was a devastating pitch. He had a limited arsenal, and it had not taken him long to learn the benefits of throwing off a hitter's timing. His changeup, which he had learned from former Reds pitcher Mario Soto, was considered one of the game's best. He used it repeatedly against the Pirates, worked out of several jams, then turned a 1–0 lead over to Pena in the ninth. Pittsburgh manager Jim Leyland countered by sending Gary Varsho, a left-handed hitter, to the plate, and he slapped a ground ball at Lemke for the first out. Jay Bell followed with a single into left field, and with the left-handed Andy Van Slyke due next, Nixon took several steps into left center field, figuring he would not pull the ball. What came next defied gravity—and the imagination.

Van Slyke launched Pena's pitch toward the right center field wall and Pendleton watched with dismay as it rose into the night.

"I thought when I saw it hit that we were going to have to come back and score two runs," he said later.

The instant Van Slyke's bat met the ball, Nixon was off, charging at an angle across the outfield, the wall looming as he sprinted, his eyes locked on the white speck cast against the night sky. At first glance, he admitted later, "I thought it was a home run." But he continued tearing across the grass, and two strides from the warning track he snuck a peek at the wall, then picked up the ball again as it began its descent. Still sprinting, he crossed the track and jumped at the wall, planting his left spike firmly in the padding, using it as leverage to lift himself higher. Up he rose, higher, higher, his glove extending a full foot over the 10-foot wall, his eyes focused on the ball. He looked like a spider, dangling from an invisible thread, seeming to linger at the peak of his jump, awaiting the ball. It disappeared over the wall, part of his glove vanished in search of it, and as gravity claimed him, he spread his legs and looked for a landing. He came down in a crouch and for a moment the crowd hushed, not sure if he had caught the ball.

Springing erect, Nixon reached into his glove and pulled out the ball, a magician flourishing a rabbit yanked from a hat, and flung it toward the infield.

"He caught the ball, he caught the ball," broadcaster Skip Caray screamed into his microphone.

Justice, circling in front of the wall, hoping to field the carom, couldn't believe his eyes.

"Awesome," he shouted at Nixon. "That was the most awesome catch I've ever seen."

Bream felt the same way. Watching from his station at first base, he recalled what his six-year-old son Mike yelled when he became excited.

"Cowabunga!" he shouted.

Regaining its voice, the crowd shook the stadium with a roar. Van Slyke, already in his home run trot, stared toward center field in disbelief.

"Otis made the best play I've ever seen in my life," Justice said later.

Turning to watch the replay on the Matrix board in center field, Nixon tipped his cap to the crowd, which continued a thunderous ovation. The end of the game was anticlimactic. Mercker came on, got Bonds to bounce out, and the Braves streamed past the mound, ignoring him, to reach Nixon.

"I watched Willie Mays make those kind of plays and I've always said I wanted to make them too," he said. "It was the best catch I've ever made."

The next day a sign, hung from the upper reaches of the stadium, captured in two words what would become known in Atlanta simply as "The Catch." The banner read "AIR NIXON."

Which would he choose, baseball or football? The deadline for Sanders's decision had drawn near and the Falcons had added to his dilemma by offering a $1 million bonus if he showed up in camp on time. Privately, Sanders shrugged at the bonus. Added to his $750,000 salary, it came to less than the $2 million he wanted to play in the NFL this season, so there was no doubt in his mind he would turn down their offer. The negotiations between Sanders and the two teams had dragged on for months, with one proposal after another offered and rejected. The Braves had wanted to keep Sanders during the week and lend him to the Falcons on weekends, a proposal the Falcons quickly shot down. The Braves had indicated they would be happy with the same arrangement Sanders had made last year, practicing with the Falcons during the day and helicoptering to their games at night. The Falcons were not interested. They wanted their All-Pro cornerback back full time.

"He's a tremendously important guy to us and we want him here and need him here," Falcons president Taylor Smith said.

Sanders enjoyed the tug-of-war for his services. He and Parker had played the two teams off against each other to increase the offers, though they still had not been able to work out an agreement with either. Schuerholz wanted to sign him to a multiyear deal, excluding football, while the Falcons wanted him to turn all his attention to football. Sanders accompanied the Braves to San Francisco still unsure of what he would do. The Falcons would not budge from their bonus offer and add to his salary, which really did not matter to him because he was not interested in participating in training camp and playing in preseason games anyway. However, no progress had been made in negotiations with the Braves either, and Sanders just wanted to get away from everything for a while.

A friend—rap star Hammer—lent Sanders a stretch limousine and invited him to visit his mansion-under-construction in San Jose. Sanders and Nixon accepted and spent the day at the house, arriving back just in time for batting practice before the game against the Giants. During the day, Sanders had reached a decision: Although Parker and Schuerholz still had not reached a compromise on a new contract, he decided to spurn the Falcons and stay with the Braves indefinitely, a decision he announced as he stood in front of his locker, encircled by reporters. It had not been a difficult choice. After all, which would he rather do, put on pads and a helmet and work out in humid, sticky conditions in Suwanee, the site of the Falcons' training camp north of Atlanta, or continue spending his evenings playing for the Braves? Sanders had decided he would remain a baseball player, at least for the moment.

"Staying indefinitely means you leave when you want," he said. "There's no reason to leave and go fishing now. We're in a pennant race and it's not fair to leave at this point."

At what point would it be fair to leave? Sanders offered no hints about the answer to that question. Schuerholz hoped it would not be before the Braves had the world championship in hand.

# AUGUST

**Pete Smith** had walked away from the Braves in June not caring if he ever returned. He had been disgusted with Cox for recalling him from Richmond and then not using him, and he had left embittered and wishing the club would trade him. He wondered if he had any future in the Braves organization. He had lost a battle with Mike Bielecki during spring training to be the fifth starter and returned to Richmond sullen and confused. Although his shoulder was sound, the Braves plainly had no confidence in him and he didn't want to stay with them. He hoped for a trade and several teams expressed interest, but Schuerholz had been reluctant to part with him. Smith's anger had increased after he was recalled in June and sat around for three weeks, appearing in one game. When he was told he would return to Richmond he considered calling his agent to insist on a trade.

"All I am is insurance for them," he raged. "An extra pitcher in case something happens. Why don't they just trade me?"

By August 1, Schuerholz was glad he had not accepted an offer for Smith. Bielecki had come off the mound feeling intense pain in his elbow during his last start and a subsequent examination revealed a torn ligament. He would miss the remainder of the season, and Smith was recalled to replace him in the rotation. It was fitting that his first start would be in a doubleheader at Candlestick Park, because in a game there two years before he had been struck on the side of the head by a line drive off Terry Kennedy's bat and his career had fizzled ever since.

He had returned from Richmond a wiser and more mature pitcher. Knowing his fastball had lost some velocity, he had worked to polish a curve and changeup and he surprised the Giants with his refurbished weapons. Will Clark struck out the first two times he faced him and the increased confidence Smith felt helped him pitch out of three jams late in the game. Holding a 1–0 lead, he stranded a runner at third base in three straight innings, and when the Braves scored twice in the top of the ninth he had his first major-league win in more than a year.

"It's been a long road back," Smith said. "It's ironic that when my career stopped it was right here, when I got hit in the head. I had a little bit more incentive to go out there and pitch well."

The trip to San Francisco illustrated the Braves' problems with being in the West division. After closing a six-game homestand against the Pirates and Astros, they flew to the West Coast for a five-game series with the Giants. Following Sunday's doubleheader at Candlestick Park, they would fly back to Atlanta and open a 10-game homestand against the Reds, Dodgers, and Padres. It was a preposterous schedule, and what made it worse was that they didn't even receive frequent flyer miles.

After the Braves lost two of the first three games to the Giants and fell into second place, Smith's performance in the first game of the doubleheader buoyed the team. Their bats suddenly awakened and they completed a sweep with an 8–5 victory in the second game. Offering a tired smile afterward, Cox said, "It's hard to win a doubleheader any time, much less here." Cox didn't realize it, but the Braves and Giants had played 18 doubleheaders at the Stick since 1966, and the Braves had swept just one.

"I can't believe we swept them," Justice said. "Everybody on this team hates playing here. If you have to play a doubleheader, you certainly don't want to do it in San Francisco. This was real big."

Brian Hunter had grown increasingly angry at his lack of playing time. He started only against left-handed pitchers, while Bream, who had half as many homers and only three more RBIs in 70 more at-bats, received most of the starts. Hunter figured Cox had taken a dislike to him, though he couldn't explain why, and the two men hardly ever spoke, except to occasionally mutter a greeting while passing in the clubhouse. The season could not end soon enough for Hunter, who wanted to hop the first flight to his Long Beach home, prop his feet up, and await the expansion draft.

"It's very frustrating," he said. "I'm the only one on the club who will sit out six games in a row. I don't know what that tells you. But I'll tell you what: If the Braves don't protect me in the expansion draft they're going to see what I can do playing every day."

Tommy Gregg shared Hunter's anger. After he recovered from the broken hand he suffered in spring training, he was sent to Richmond on a rehabilitation assignment, then was left there because the Braves did not have a roster spot available. He felt like the invisible man, unseen and unwanted by the team. He was finally recalled when it appeared Sanders might rejoin the Falcons, flew to San Francisco to meet the team, then was left to stew in the clubhouse over the weekend when Sanders decided he would stay. Gregg had had enough. Like Hunter, he wanted out, and the sooner the better.

Gregg had thought he would be recalled earlier to add a left-handed bat to the bench, but Cox was unwilling to dump Lonnie Smith or Treadway to make room for him. A former punt returner and wide receiver at Wake Forest, Gregg saw his stock with the Braves plummet so quickly he was left shaking his head. Just two years ago, at age 26, he had been the game's best pinch hitter, a role he had initially felt uncomfortable in but eventually came to enjoy. Still hopeful of becoming a regular, he had been prepared to endure another season on the bench in 1991, but he suffered a broken hand in April of that year. When he returned in June he couldn't find his stroke and finished with a .187 average. Cox had paid little attention to him since then.

"I don't know why I'm in the doghouse," Gregg said. "I can't explain it. I don't know why I'm being swept under the rug. That's why I can't wait to leave. I'm hoping and praying that one of those expansion teams picks me so I can get the hell out of this organization."

It was difficult to understand why Cox was considered a "player's manager" when he had so many players unhappy with their situations. He was not a rah-rah type, he enforced a strict policy forbidding wearing earrings on the field (even as friends of many Braves on opposing teams displayed their earrings around the batting cage), and he was one of the few remaining managers who maintained a curfew on the road. While he wasn't buddy-buddy with the players, he wasn't a distant, unapproachable presence in the clubhouse either. If players liked him it was because he never ripped them in the media, no matter how severe their sins, and was tolerant of their cellular phones in the clubhouse and their putting contests before games. Cox had mellowed over the years, though an umpire's call could still raise his ire, and his ideals remained rooted in the 1940s.

He grew up in Fresno, California, and earned money as a boy working under a broiling sun picking grapes and strawberries for pennies an hour. He was a talented athlete and was offered football scholarships to several colleges, but accepted a $40,000 bonus to sign with the Los Angeles Dodgers. A third baseman, he eventually reached the major leagues with the New York Yankees in 1968, but was there for only two seasons before bad knees forced him to quit. He turned to managing and in six years in the minors never had a losing season. Hidden beneath the calm expression he wore in the dugout lay a fiery competitor, and his aggressive nature often resulted in a smashed toilet or dented doors following a loss. He took over a dreadful Braves team in 1978 and two years later guided them to an 81–80 record. The improvement wasn't good enough for Turner, who fired Cox after the 1981 season with the team poised on the brink of a championship season, a decision he almost instantly regretted. At a news conference announcing Cox's dismissal, Turner was asked what qualities he would seek in a new manager.

"If Bobby Cox weren't [sitting] here and we were looking for a new manager, he'd be one of the leading candidates," he replied.

Since then, Cox had won a division championship in Toronto, then returned to the Braves as general manager, a role for which he was ill-suited. He was a nice guy in a job that at times required someone with no conscience, his loyalty to players sometimes overriding good business sense. He couldn't bring himself to trade Dale Murphy until his value had decreased to a point where he had to be practically given away, a necessary deal that still left Cox feeling miserable. He didn't feel any more comfortable firing manager Russ Nixon in 1990, especially since Nixon had been his choice as manager two years before. He had named himself to replace Nixon and knew immediately it was the right decision. Being in the clubhouse six or seven hours before game time, a pinch of tobacco in his cheek and a lineup card in front of him, was as comforting to Cox as having his old infielder's mitt lying nearby. He knew the dugout was where he belonged and he wouldn't make the mistake of leaving it again.

Although the game had not changed since Cox played, the players had. He was now dealing with players making five and six times as much money as he did, players with egos that blossomed and spread like mushroom clouds, and media that scrutinized every detail from salaries to strategy. He maintained an approach inside the clubhouse he had learned from former Yankees manager Ralph Houk, a man he admired for the way he treated his players.

"He showed a little more compassion for players than others," Cox said. "These guys are human. You don't wind them up and turn them loose all the time."

Cox liked the focus to be on the players. He was happy to remain in the background. He was fidgety and uncomfortable in the glare of television lights and often hid out in the bullpen before games rather than talk with reporters and face camera crews. However, sitting in the dugout hours before a game, long before most writers arrived and the stadium gates opened, he was a different person. Cox loved to listen to stories, whether it was another of Yost's hunting tales or Mazzone's yarns about life in the Mexican League, and he would often laugh so hard tears came to his eyes. Comfortable in surroundings as familiar to him as his own living room, he would open up and talk about his daughter Skyla's softball team or reminisce about his days with the Yankees or speak excitedly about the cabin he had bought in the woods of northern Georgia. Cox didn't often provide glimpses into his life away from the ballpark. When he did, he revealed a man holding the same dreams and aspirations as any other husband and father.

First place was at stake when the Reds arrived in Atlanta for a sold-out three-game series. The Braves led the division by a half-game and would send their top three starters, Glavine, Avery, and Smoltz, to the mound, while Cincinnati countered with Tom Bolton, Tim Belcher, and Greg Swindell. Although two months remained in the season, the series was considered pivotal by both teams, who would face each other just five more times the rest of the way. Piniella was upbeat as he settled into his office in the visitors' clubhouse, happy to add third baseman Chris Sabo and left fielder Reggie Sanders to the lineup after injuries had caused each to miss games. He and Cox got along, both being former Yankees, but the Reds manager wasn't above a bit of psychological warfare to attempt to gain an edge. Knowing his comments would find their way into the home clubhouse, he told writers before the game that the Braves were feeling more pressure than the Reds, because they were expected to win the division.

"I think there is a little more heat on Atlanta," he said. "Just about everybody has conceded the division to them."

Told later of Piniella's words, Cox shook his head and chuckled.

"I'd rather be the one out front than the one who's chasing," he said.

The first game was the most important one of the series. It would set the tone for the remaining games and increase the pressure on the losing team to take the final two. The Reds jumped on Glavine early, taking a 2–0 lead after three innings, and they led 5–2 in the eighth. Bolton and a pair of relievers had little trouble with the Braves, limiting them to three hits in seven innings. Needing six outs to jump back into first place, Piniella called on Charlton, who had 24 saves, including a pair against the Braves, to lock it up. Unlike last season, when they seemed to pull off a miracle finish every other week, the Braves had managed few comebacks this year. In the dugout Pendleton felt a sinking sensation in his stomach as he watched Charlton march to the mound.

"They had one of the best relievers in the game," he said later. "If I was just an observer I would have said it's awful tough [to win] because they have Charlton on the mound."

Yet, before Charlton could retire the side in the eighth the Braves had tied the game. Pendleton provided an RBI single, Justice drove in a run with a double, and Olson pushed across the tying run with a sacrifice fly, all coming on 0-and-2 pitches. Charlton was struggling, especially with his forkball, which he couldn't keep down in the strike zone, but Piniella sent him back out to the mound in the ninth. He got two quick outs before he walked Nixon, who promptly stole second. Pendleton was next and he approached the plate thinking Charlton would walk him to face Gant, still mired hopelessly in a slump, and was surprised when catcher Joe Oliver returned to his crouch behind the plate. Charlton missed the strike zone with two of his first three pitches and, figuring Pendleton was looking for a fastball, he threw a forkball, hoping he would top it to one of his infielders. The instant the ball left his hand Charlton knew he had made a mistake. The pitch wallowed to the plate like a ship taking on water and Pendleton belted it high over the left field wall, his second game-winning, bottom-of-the-ninth homer in two months.

"I'm not trying to be arrogant or cocky," Pendleton said after the game. "But if it had been me pitching, I would have been more careful with myself."

Said Blauser, "That win was like déjà vu, reminiscent of some games we had last year."

Piniella, who was often criticized by the Cincinnati press for his poor judgment, was furious at himself for leaving Charlton in the game. He knew he should have used the hard-throwing Rob Dibble to face Olson in the eighth inning or gone to him in the ninth, but he had acted tentatively, in contrast to his usually aggressive style. Approached by reporters after the game and questioned about his decisions, a livid Piniella snapped, "You saw what happened. Just write it. What the hell am I going to tell you guys?"

The next night the Reds received another jolt when Roberts, their diminutive center fielder and leadoff hitter, crashed face-first into the center field wall chasing Justice's triple in the first inning. He remained prone for 15 minutes and when he left the field on a stretcher the Reds gulped nervously and thought to themselves, "What's going to happen next?" In short order, they found out. The Braves won the final two games and seized a three-and-a-half-game lead, their largest division lead since 1983, and the Reds exited dejected and despairing.

"I guess we'll have to start watching the scoreboard," Swindell said quietly.

Looking back on the series later, Reds general manager Bob Quinn pinpointed the exact moment his club lost the division race. He felt it was the instant Pendleton's homer disappeared beyond the left field wall in the first game.

"The most pivotal loss of the season," Quinn said. "The momentum from that game was like a tidal wave."

A rush of confidence surged through Atlanta's clubhouse. The Braves felt the Reds were teetering and with a little push could topple out of the race. Their mood was best reflected by Olson, who suggested, "The division is pretty much ours to lose."

The last time Dodgers manager Tommy Lasorda was in Atlanta he had taken a walk one afternoon outside the stadium and been heckled good-naturedly by some of the neighborhood residents who wanted to see the Braves sweep his team.

"Three in a row, Tommy," a boy had yelled.

Lasorda had laughed and stopped to talk and before long a crowd had gathered. Never one to pass on an opportunity to test the power of his vocal cords, he had displayed the vigor of a street preacher, his voice raised and his hands gesturing emphatically.

"Don't you realize the Dodgers are the organization that gave Jackie Robinson his opportunity?" he said, his voice beginning to boom. "You should be yelling 'I love the Dodgers, I love the Dodgers.' "

Continuing, Lasorda recounted the Dodgers' past triumphs and held the group spellbound. When he departed a few minutes later, the crowd was chanting, "I love the Dodgers, I love the Dodgers." Relating the story later, Lasorda had chuckled and said, "I had a good time. They're good people."

Two months later he returned dragging a rag-tag collection of ballplayers with him. The Dodgers weren't just bad, they were horrible, owners of one of the worst records in either league, and Lasorda was so unhappy he was unsure whether he wanted to return to the dugout next season. The crowd at the stadium did not seem willing to kick him when he was down. Last season's passion—the "Beat L.A." chants and anti-Lasorda signs—had disappeared, replaced by a politeness that bordered on pity for a once-proud team now disgraced by failure. The Dodgers played flat, like a team already planning its winter activities, and even Lasorda's exuberance couldn't lift them from the doldrums.

"When you have guys like [Darryl] Strawberry and [Eric] Davis hurt, it takes the wind out of a ballclub," Nixon said. "They're a different team than what we saw last year."

Pendleton wanted to make sure the Braves didn't take the Dodgers lightly. During a brief meeting before the first game of the series he reminded everyone to maintain their focus and not suffer a letdown after sweeping the Reds. He need not have worried. The Braves won three of four games, outscored the Dodgers 31–12, and moved four games in front of the Reds. Only Sanders emerged from the weekend unhappy. He had hoped he would start Saturday afternoon's game, which was CBS's national telecast, and when he saw his name missing from the lineup he was furious.

His face stormy and his voice rising, he said, "What does a nigger have to do to get on CBS? I might as well leave and go get my hair done. Man, I told everyone I was playing today."

Sanders had been so sure he would start he had spread the word among his friends to tune in the telecast and watch him play. When he became angry he occasionally flung the word "nigger" about, a word that was acceptable in the clubhouse if spoken by a black player.

Lemke's problem paled in comparison to Sanders's woes. At least Lemke played in Saturday's game, though he almost missed the first pitch. When he had not arrived in the clubhouse 45 minutes before the start of the game, his teammates exchanged knowing glances, figuring he had forgotten it was an afternoon game, but that wasn't the case. He had been delayed at home when the battery in his truck died and by the time he reached the exit to the stadium, traffic clogged the streets. Mired in a bumper-to-bumper jam, with the stadium looming in the distance, Lemke rolled down the window of his truck and asked a motorcycle policeman to give him a lift. The officer refused.

"It's amazing how much traffic was out there," Lemke said later. "I didn't know what I was going to do. I was wondering if it would ever clear out in front of the stadium."

Lemke finally reached the clubhouse with a half-hour to spare, scrambled into his uniform, then went out and collected three hits and scored a pair of runs in the Braves' 12–2 win.


Lonnie Smith had given up hope of being traded. He had seen the Giants trade veteran outfielder Kevin Bass to the New York Mets for a player to be named later and couldn't understand why a similar deal could not be worked out between the Braves and a team in need of a hitter. He had waited patiently for months for Schuerholz to ship him out, and when no deal was made he became resigned to finishing the season in Atlanta.

"You can only try to make things happen for so long," he said.

The Braves had made no such deal because Cox had no intention of letting him go. He considered Smith his best pinch hitter and a consistent threat in clutch situations, a hitter still able to turn on a fastball as quickly as much younger players. However, Smith remained unhappy with his lack of playing time. He felt uncomfortable coming to the plate only a handful of times each week and was fearful he had already been slapped with a can't-play-every-day label by other teams in the league. That wasn't his only concern. His contract expired after the season and he wondered if there would be any jobs available for an outfielder who would turn 37 before the first pitch of the new season was made.

"It's hard to say where I'm going to go or what's going to happen," he said. "There's a possibility this is my last season. I'd like to not think that way, but you just have to prepare for it the best way you can."

An air of melancholy clung to Smith. He had the sad and weary eyes of someone who had peered into a pit of demons and dragged himself away from the edge, knowing the hole remained uncovered and inviting behind him. There was no escaping his past: the stay in a drug rehabilitation center, his role as a witness in the Pittsburgh baseball drug trials, his subsequent release by the Royals, his career apparently over at age 32. He had fought his way back from cocaine addiction, a habit he once admitted led him to "screw up a good part of my life," a dark secret he exorcised at immeasurable cost.

"It started as a way of just hanging out and carried over into an addiction," he said. "I started doing it during the season, as well as doing it twice as much during the off-season. It becomes a big problem, a financial problem as well as a problem where you just escape from all the realities and the responsibilities. You become more dependent on the drug than anything else."

The commissioner's office had tested him regularly and he had remained clean for nine years. However, the demons, Smith admitted a couple of years ago, still lingered behind him, waiting for him to drop his guard.

"I'm not cured," he said. "It can still happen. When you're alone, when you're getting restless, bored, you want to do something. It's a little dangerous at times. Sometimes you get to thinking and it's along the wrong line of thinking. This is a battle I have to fight all my life."

Even with a pair of expansion teams beginning play next year, Smith knew the odds of his catching on with another club were not good. His salary and his age were two big deterrents. Like Hunter, he planned to be in front of his television set to watch the expansion draft, not because he thought he might be selected but to determine which team would be the best one to approach. His career was winding down and he was reluctant to let it end.

"I don't necessarily try and savor every moment, I just try to have fun every day," he said. "Winning helps a lot. If we were losing it would be different."

But winning or not, fun was in as short supply as his at-bats lately, and his athlete's equivalent of the biological clock was ticking very loudly.

The artillery in the heart of the Braves' lineup had the pop of cap pistols. Gant and Justice continued to flounder at the plate, unable to duplicate the power they had demonstrated in the past two years, and each had already dismissed the season and was looking ahead. At different times each player had privately vowed to work harder during the winter and report to spring training in the best condition of his career. Justice had admitted he had relaxed last winter and did not prepare as diligently as he had in the past, partly because he was protecting his troublesome back. His futile at-bats mounted as quickly as his count of discarded batting stances, and he became more and more worried and sank deeper into the abyss. He and Gant had combined for two home runs in their last 342 at-bats; Lemke had three in just the last 10 games.

"My whole thing is I'm trying to hit twenty homers in one at-bat," Justice said. "Right now when I get a pitch I can drive I try and hit it out instead of just hitting it hard. My whole approach has always been to hit the ball hard on the ground and the home runs will come. But when you get into the approach of trying to hit every ball out, that's when you go down."

Gant had given up on reaching 30–30 in a third straight season. He had awakened one morning with the realization that his dream had died and no matter how hot he became there was no chance he would reach his goal.

"I'm to the point now where I know it's damn near impossible to do," he said sadly. "I definitely wanted to do it, I just wasn't able to."

Gant remained confused and tense at the plate, unable to incorporate the advice Mays offered him at the All-Star game into his approach. Jones had become impatient with him and one day behind the batting cage he had railed at him for taking negative thoughts to the plate. The hitting coach felt Gant had allowed minor distractions to contribute to his slide and he pushed him to start becoming more aggressive and not to allow one poor at-bat to spoil his next three or four plate appearances. It was a habit Gant found hard to break. He would often throw his helmet after hitting a ground ball or toss his bat after popping up, and would brood about it through the rest of the game.

"Physically, C.J. can help me in every way," Gant said. "But mentally, I've got to do it myself. That's what I'm working on right now. I'm trying to stay positive."

Cox began to think Gant might not shake his slump and he decided he couldn't afford to keep his flailing bat in the lineup. While insisting he was not starting another platoon, he began to rotate Sanders and Smith in left field, leaving Gant on the bench three or four times a week. Gant didn't like it, but he was in no position to argue.

"We're in a pennant race and the team needs me really bad, that's probably the most frustrating thing," he said. "I'm feeling like I'm really letting the team down. Going through something like this makes you realize how important it is to keep working and not get complacent."

With the offense needing a spark, Cox turned to Smith. He decided to give Justice a night off as the Braves opened a seven-game trip in Pittsburgh, and Smith responded with one of the most memorable games of his career. Before a glowing yellow moon had a chance to rise above Three Rivers Stadium, Smith hit a grand slam in the second inning, his first since hitting one against Nolan Ryan in 1984, and the Braves roared to a 15–0 victory. Smith entered the game with a .213 batting average, but after a five-hit, six-RBI performance, he exited with a .259 average.

"It will go down as my best game as a Brave," he said. "It goes right into the memory banks."

The Braves continued to play well. They had won 8 of their last 10 games to increase their lead over the Reds to 5½ games, their largest advantage of the season. The offense, even with

Gant and Justice struggling, was near the top of the league in batting average and runs scored. Pendleton was hitting .310 and Nixon was hot, but the most pleasant surprise was the return of Bream's bat. He and Yost had been quietly working on the side to adjust his swing and now, Bream said, "I have a better idea of what I'm trying to do up there." He was in the middle of a stretch where he would drive in 11 runs in 14 games, and his confidence began to soar. He went to the plate relaxed and feeling comfortable, and his stroke was smooth and rhythmic.

"It's just like in golf," Bream said. "When you're swinging well you don't have to swing hard to get the ball to jump."

Jeff Treadway had reached a decision. Like Blauser he had become fearful of being labeled a utility player and he felt his career had stalled following his recovery from hand surgery. He decided to seek a trade. It was a painful decision because he had grown up watching the Braves and enjoyed having family and friends make the trip from Griffin to see him play. However, he was convinced Cox had settled on Lemke as his regular second baseman and he felt he had no future with the team.

"My main point is I'm not ready to fall into a utility or pinch-hitting role," Treadway said. "I know there's too much left in me for that to happen. I think I can be a starting second baseman for the next four or five years with no problem."

A quiet man who kept largely to himself, he directed his agent to discuss a trade with Schuerholz, who responded with a "we'll see what we can do." Treadway wasn't willing to wait. He felt it was important to show another team what he could do so he could be included in their plans next season, but Schuerholz balked at his impatient approach. He was annoyed the second baseman would demand a trade when the team was playing so well, and he was leery of creating a distraction that could disrupt the club. He made it clear to Treadway he didn't plan on making a change.

"I don't think this is very appropriate timing, as far as the team interests are concerned," he said. "You don't have to be overt about your dissatisfaction to create a negative vibe around you."

But Treadway—like Hunter and Berenguer and Sanders and Smith and the other unhappy Braves—didn't want to hear about "team interests." Though he was generally uncomfortable talking with reporters and never sought the spotlight, Treadway began a war of words with the general manager in the newspapers. Although he rarely displayed anger, he became incensed after he learned Schuerholz had rebuffed his trade demand. He criticized him for what he felt was an uncaring attitude, saying, "When the general manager comes out and says he's not concerned about an individual, then that means I'm the only one who cares about Jeff Treadway and his future. He says he doesn't care about me and that's part of the problem I have with him. It's just another negative. Now you know why I feel the way I feel."

However, there was little Treadway or his agent could do to force a trade. And more balanced observers couldn't see any reason why the Braves should put Jeff Treadway's interests ahead of the team's. Cox felt it was important to have Treadway around in case Lemke was injured, and he also provided another left-handed pinch hitter on the bench. With no suitable backup to Lemke ready in the minor leagues, Schuerholz would not deal away Treadway without receiving a comparable player in return. Treadway was stuck and he knew it. While he remained with the team, playing once or twice a week, he smoldered each time Schuerholz entered the clubhouse. After being the club's regular second baseman for two years he no longer felt like part of the team and he wondered if his career had begun a slow fade to black. Like the others, he was looking past September and October to November's expansion draft.

"I would welcome an expansion team drafting me with open arms," he said. "It would be an opportunity to play."

.   .   .

Ned Yost fit in better with the players than with the coaching staff. Just 37, he wasn't much older than Lonnie Smith and Leibrandt and he related well to all the players. It was his clothes they took exception to. A former catcher with the Milwaukee Brewers and Texas Rangers, Ned Yost had not been in the major leagues in six years when he was named the bullpen coach in 1991, and his wardrobe was well behind the times. Like most teams, the Braves required players to wear coats and ties on road trips, a rule that gave everyone a chance to show off. Everyone except Yost. His collection of suitable clothes was so meager he looked like Jed Clampett alongside the fashionably attired players.

"I'm a T-shirt and jeans guy," he admitted.

It took little coaxing to get Yost, an avid hunter, to produce photos of trophy bucks he had shot, and he looked forward to returning to the woods each fall. He had more camouflage in his closet than Savile Row. Yost and his wardrobe had become a running joke among the players and he finally tired of it, visiting a men's shop and spending $1,500 on coats, shirts, pants, and ties. But even with the new duds, he still felt like Tarzan preparing for a night out on the town. During a road trip earlier in the season he had sat in his hotel room attempting to match his shirts with ties and his coats with his shirts and his pants with everything, and finally he had flung his hands up in disgust.

"It was hopeless," he said.

He returned all the clothes to the men's shop and asked for help. Using a computer, the owner figured every possible combination for him, about 350 in all, then gave him a printout of the information so he could make up his own little book. Yost numbered and lettered his ties, shirts, pants, and coats, and before each road trip he thumbed through his guide to find the proper combinations to pack.

"I'll be perfectly color-coordinated from here on out," he promised.

.   .   .

As always, Otis Nixon enjoyed the road stop in Montreal, where he was still a fan favorite. He had made an effort to fit in with the culture while he was there, learning enough French to get by, and many of the Expos and stadium workers greeted him like a long-lost brother when the Braves arrived. Like many players who have been traded away, Nixon also relished haunting his former team, as he did in a game in 1991 when he tied a major league record with six stolen bases. He looked forward to another opportunity to show the Expos how wrong they had been to trade him and was stunned to see his name missing from the lineup when he entered the clubhouse. Figuring Nixon could use a day off, Cox had penciled in Sanders to play center field and Nixon exploded.

"If I can't play when I'm hitting .340, when can I play?" he demanded. "I don't need a day off. There's nothing wrong with me. I'm not in a slump."

Cox's decision surprised many of the Braves, who privately exchanged puzzled looks after they had reviewed the lineup. Several players spoke quietly with Nixon and asked why he wasn't playing, which only increased his anger. He was particularly upset because he felt Cox had violated the agreement reached earlier in the season with him and Sanders, in which he promised to tell each player when he was starting.

"He agreed to tell Deion and me what he was doing," Nixon said. "He just feels he can pop me in and out of the lineup and I don't want to be that kind of player. I'll go somewhere else before that happens."

Nixon's attitude mirrored the frustration many players felt. The sport they had enjoyed as youngsters had changed. While baseball remained a team game, the incredible salaries owners lavished on players had helped to divide their focus. Contributing to a winning team wasn't enough anymore; owners rewarded the players with the best statistics and the only way to compile the numbers was to play regularly. Numbers mean everything in baseball, particularly the figures following a dollar sign. Treadway, Hunter, and the other part-time players all wanted to be regulars, and they became increasingly angry as they sat on the bench. Even as the Braves continued winning, they remained unhappy and concerned about their futures in the game. Their attitudes were selfish and self-centered, but in a game of millionaires, who could blame them for wanting a slice of the pie?

Cox had unwittingly struck a nerve with Nixon, who was intent on proving his success of 1991 was no fluke. He was in one of his hot streaks at the plate, with 9 hits in his last 20 at-bats, and he felt a night off would shatter his focus. As the start of the game neared and the Braves left the clubhouse to warm up and stretch, Nixon remained in front of his locker. He had decided he would not sit in the dugout and when Cox went looking for him midway through the game, he found him watching the game on television in the clubhouse. He asked him to come out to the bench and Nixon refused. They talked for a few minutes and Cox admitted, "You have a perfect right to be upset." Nixon remained in the clubhouse throughout the game as Sanders had a pair of hits and scored a run in the Braves' 5–1 win. Nixon was in the lineup the next night, so the minicrisis passed, but it was a distraction that could have been easily avoided.

During a game earlier in the season Rafael Belliard missed a suicide-squeeze bunt sign and a runner coming from third base was tagged out. Cox was asked the next day if Belliard would be fined and he had looked up in amazement.

"Fine Raffy?" he said. "He's one of the nicest guys on the team. Why would I fine him?"

That's how everyone felt about Belliard. He was their little brother, a diminutive man whose elfin features were usually crinkled at the corners by a smile. He had the same effect on a roomful of people as Norm in "Cheers." When he walked into the clubhouse everyone looked up and greeted him with a warm "Raffy!" He and Lemke usually recognized each other by knocking their forearms together, a take-off on the signature salute of Oakland's "Bash Brothers" following a home run. It was a particularly funny greeting from Belliard, who had spurred the demise of Padres pitcher Eric Show by hitting his only major league home run against him in 1987. He had been to the plate more than 1,200 times since then without hitting one out, though he came close during a game at Wrigley Field in June. He had swung mightily and lifted a fly to the warning track, then complained bitterly afterward, saying, "I hit the ball good, but the wind changed." Cubs left fielder Kal Daniels was playing deeper than most outfielders and backpedaled quickly to glove the ball.

Daniels's unusual respect for Belliard's power left the shortstop outraged. "Nobody plays me there," Belliard moaned. "What was he doing there?"

One of Schuerholz's top priorities after accepting the job as general manager was to improve the infield defense, and he had moved swiftly to grab Belliard at a bargain basement price of $875,000 for two years. The contract expired after the season, allowing Belliard to become a free agent, and Schuerholz, who didn't like to negotiate during the season, made an exception to his rule. He wanted to add two years to the contract and Belliard was eager to get it done.

"I don't look for big money," he said. "Money isn't everything. I'd rather be happy. Atlanta is a nice city and a lot of good things have happened to me here. I'm an easy guy to deal with."

Contract negotiations usually plod along at the pace of a camel caravan across the Sahara, but Schuerholz and Belliard's agent, Tom Reich, got a deal done in record time. Belliard agreed to a two-year extension for $800,000 per season, with incentives for games played that could hike his pay to $1 million per year.

"I'm happy," he said. "Now I can relax and go play."


For three months Glavine had been pitching as if he were on autopilot, reeling off a modern-day franchise record 13 consecutive wins to put himself in position to win a second straight Cy Young Award. Leading the league with 19 wins he felt vindicated. He had shown that his 20-win season in 1991 was no fluke and he took great satisfaction in having proved skeptics wrong. However, his success came at a price. Expectations had climbed so high that no matter how well he pitched, he couldn't please everyone.

"I went through this last year with everybody," he said. "If I give up two or three runs, then everybody says I had a bad game. I'm not going to be mistake-free every night."

As Glavine climbed the steps from the home dugout August 25 and headed to the bullpen mound to warm up to face the Expos, he felt butterflies begin to stir and take wing in his stomach. He always grew nervous before a start and he would have felt odd if he had reached the mound without experiencing the first twinges of excitement. As he warmed up he reviewed his last start, a 4–2 win over the Expos in Montreal, and decided he would change his tactics the second time around. He had used his curve and slider more than usual in the previous start, feeling the Expos were narrowing him down to being just a fastball-changeup pitcher, and had allowed seven hits and both runs over eight and a third innings. He decided to keep the Expos guessing by throwing his fastball more often and mixing in his other three pitches, an approach he hoped would keep them off-balance.

As he limbered up in the bullpen, Glavine felt a sudden twinge in his right side, then a sharp pain. He continued to throw but the pain intensified, a biting jab in his ribs that, he remembered later, "Took my breath away and made me sick to my stomach." Six weeks later he would ruefully admit he should not have continued pitching, but at the time he vowed that he would let no one call him a wimp. Glavine marched to the mound with a hairline fracture of a rib and the Expos battered him for seven hits and five runs in four and two-thirds innings. Lying in bed that night, he was in agony. Each breath he drew was painful and he lay awake trying to remain as still as possible.

"I couldn't breathe, couldn't move, and couldn't sleep," he

said. "I sneezed driving over to the doctor's office the next morning and it hurt so bad I almost drove off the road."

Glavine thought the origin of the injury might be traced back to July, when he fell sick in St. Louis. He had spent a night coughing and throwing up, and the rib might have weakened then. But he wasn't certain and doctors couldn't shed any light on the cause. Although Cox and Mazzone knew of his injury, Glavine refused to say anything publicly. Doctors had cleared him to pitch if he could stand the pain and he decided to continue his pursuit of a twentieth win. Later he would explain, "I didn't tell anybody because I didn't want the other teams to know. I was worried if they knew they might try to bunt on me or throw one inside when I'm at the plate."

Glavine's injury wasn't the only bad news to hit the pitching staff. Sharp pain had appeared in Pena's elbow the week before and he had walked off the mound wearing a grim expression. Doctors diagnosed the injury as tendinitis after an arthrogram revealed no tear, but he would miss at least two weeks and Schuerholz knew he had to act fast. The deadline for adding players to the roster in order to have them eligible for the postseason was in three days and if he didn't make a trade quickly the club might be stuck without a closer. Cox didn't feel comfortable turning the role over to Wohlers or Stanton, preferring a veteran for the job, and Schuerholz went to work.

He knew White Sox reliever Bobby Thigpen, Rangers stopper Jeff Russell, and Cardinals pitcher Danny Cox were available, but the teams were asking for two and three players in return and he felt that was too steep a price to pay. He and Red Sox general manager Lou Gorman were longtime friends and had talked about Reardon in July, but the talks had been shelved when Pena began pitching well. Gorman called back when word of Pena's injury reached him and offered to swap Reardon for 23-year-old Richmond second baseman Ramon Caraballo or 21-year-old outfielder Melvin Nieves, who was playing at Double-A Greenville. Schuerholz didn't bite. He knew Gorman was desperate to dump second baseman Jody Reed and find a replacement, but Caraballo was a top prospect and he wouldn't give him away for an aging reliever. Nieves was also a highly rated prospect, a switch hitter with power, and Schuerholz wouldn't trade him. Lajoie's reports on Reardon suggested he could still do the job, but Cox wasn't sold on him. While he was the general manager he had come very close to completing a trade with Gorman for closer Lee Smith and he wished he had pulled the trigger on the deal. He wanted a hard thrower, a pitcher who could come in and dominate a ninth inning, and Reardon's fastball was well past its prime. Cox sighed. Down through the years the Braves had searched in vain for a closer, a quest that had produced only two relievers with more than 25 saves in a season since 1966. Reardon was not Cox's first choice, but he would have to do.

"There wasn't much left out there, not for a decent price," said a Braves scout. "When you go down the stretch you probably take a shot at someone you normally wouldn't."

Schuerholz told Gorman he would be willing to part with a pair of minor league players, Richmond outfielder Sean Ross and Class AA Greenville pitcher Nate Minchey, knowing he wouldn't be able to protect them in the expansion draft anyway. Gorman, who had no plans to re-sign Reardon, studied his scouting reports on the pair and decided to accept the deal.

Delighted, Reardon said, "I look at it as being the biggest break of my career. I could have gone out and saved 45 or 50 games this year and I don't think the Red Sox would have signed me back. I'm not exactly young, but I know I can still pitch."

The acquisition of Reardon bolstered spirits in the Braves bullpen. With Pena out, the relievers had been shifted into different and uncomfortable roles. An unchallenged closer allowed Cox to manage an eight-inning game and turn the ninth over to Reardon.

As Olson would say later, "For those guys down there [in the bullpen], you go from a team that doesn't have a real

Bill Zack

proven closer to all of a sudden the save leader of all time. Once he came over, all that pressure on those guys was released. Suddenly, they didn't have to do someone else's job anymore. They just had to get it to the ninth."

With their new closer in place and holding a six-and-a-half-game lead over Cincinnati, the Braves felt fully ready to take that one step further than last year's postseason allowed them.

The Braves finished their last-minute roster shuffle by recalling catcher Francisco Cabrera from Richmond, a move that made him eligible for postseason play. Cabrera was a good hitter, but he lacked the defensive skills to be a regular catcher. Though he probably wouldn't need one, Cox felt more comfortable with a third catcher on the potential playoff roster, and Cabrera would provide an extra bat coming off the bench.

# SEPTEMBER

As Manhattan's skyscrapers rose in the distance the Braves groaned. They hated New York with a passion, couldn't stand its teeming streets and $25 continental breakfasts, and looked forward to leaving before they had even arrived.

"It's too bad that we have to come here," Pendleton grumbled.

Cox had once seen a man die of stab wounds on a Manhattan sidewalk and the players had run across enough weirdos, wackos, and crazies to keep everyone pinned in their hotel rooms until the bus departed for Shea Stadium in Queens each afternoon. A few adventuresome players occasionally braved the subway to reach Shea and some daring others hailed cabs, which Mercker and Avery had found could be an expensive undertaking. Fresh to the big leagues in 1990, the pair jumped into a taxi and discovered the driver didn't speak English.

"Shea Stadium," Mercker explained patiently. "We want to go to Shea Stadium. You know, where the Mets play."

Nodding his head, the cabbie sped off and the two players

settled back and relaxed. A half-hour later the taxi pulled over to a curb and Mercker looked up in horror at Yankee Stadium.

"It only cost us about $290,000 to finally get to Shea," he remembered later.

Leibrandt was with the Reds in the early 1980s when he and five or six other players hopped a subway to Shea. He had opened a newspaper and was deep in the sports pages when he was startled by a pounding and shouting outside the car. Looking up, he was aghast to see his teammates, who had gotten up to change trains, standing outside beckoning to him. Before he could react, the doors closed and he was left standing there, somewhat panicked, as the train pulled away from the platform. Leibrandt got off at the next stop and approached the cashier's booth to ask directions and discovered the attendant didn't speak English.

"I made it back, but it was a little hairy," he recalled.

No trip to New York would be complete without at least one odd happening, and the Braves received their first jolt before they had even reached the hotel lobby. Stepping from the team bus, coach Jim Beauchamp felt something give way in his left knee and a jolt of pain surged through his leg. Instead of going up to his room and relaxing, he headed to St. Vincent's Hospital, accompanied by Dr. Chandler, the club's orthopedist. Beauchamp, a bear of a man with a drawl of pure southern molasses, was horror-stricken at the chaotic scene inside the emergency room. As Chandler remembered it later, the two men walked in and recoiled at the spectacle.

"There were people taking napkins out of their pockets to turn doorknobs and one of the first things we saw was a woman with needle marks all over her arm," Chandler said. "Jim wanted to get out of there."

Seated and waiting for a doctor, Beauchamp became increasingly nervous as the hectic pace continued and the room filled with people. When a doctor finally approached and began to lead him toward an X-ray room, Beauchamp looked back at a still-seated Chandler and wailed, "Don't leave me!"

Later, after X-rays had revealed he would need major surgery to repair the damage, Beauchamp had remarked, "If I was a horse, they'd shoot me."

Back at the hotel, Blauser visited Beauchamp's room to commiserate with him and they ordered a six-pack of beer from room service. When it was delivered the waiter handed Blauser the bill to sign; the player's jaw dropped when he saw a charge of $28.

"Paying that much, I thought I was buying stock in the company," he said.

David Nied stepped from the dugout, looked around Shea Stadium and his mouth gaped open. If he had not quite believed he was in the big leagues before, he did now. The ballpark in Richmond paled in comparison to Shea. A monstrous scoreboard towered above the right field wall and the grandstands rose like giant sentinels along both lines. The dramatic effect was further enhanced by the regular roar of jets passing overhead on their final approach to LaGuardia Airport, located only a mile or two away. Nied, an earnest and likable youngster of 23, shook his head in bewilderment. He had been recalled by the Braves when rosters expanded to 40 players September 1, and he would make his major league debut the same day. Cox liked having rookie pitchers debut on the road. He thought it lessened the pressure, not having to pitch in front of a home crowd, and he had been proven right. Glavine had debuted in Houston, Smoltz in New York, and Avery in Cincinnati and each pitcher had remarked later that he felt more comfortable in subsequent starts having opened away from home.

Nonetheless, Nied felt jittery. He was astonished at the size of Shea—"I've never pitched in something as big as this before"—and wondered if he was ready for this moment. Standing on the mound in the bottom of the first inning he felt the butterflies swarming in his stomach. He shivered as he considered that the eyes of his parents and assorted other rela-

tives, who had made the trip from his hometown of Duncan-
ville, Texas, were fastened on him.

"I felt uncomfortable, like I didn't belong," he admitted
later.

Vince Coleman led off with a double and scored. Eddie
Murray and Bobby Bonilla drew two-out walks and Mazzone
trotted to the mound and stared into the young pitcher's face.

"You've got good, live stuff," he assured him. "And you've
got a great defense behind you. Let them help you out."

Still struggling to corral his butterflies, Nied nodded. He
went back to work and escaped the inning without further
damage, then swept through the next six, allowing three hits
and no more runs. When he departed after making 106
pitches in seven innings, the Braves led 4–1 in a game they
would win by that score and Nied breathed a huge sigh of
relief.

"I didn't want to disappoint my family after they made the
trip up here," he said. "But I know I won't sleep a wink tonight."

Early the next morning Nied hurried out of the hotel and
was pulling change out of his pocket before he even reached
the newspaper stand on the corner. He bought a half-dozen
papers and, grinning, cheerfully acknowledged that "I'll probably have them framed."

Like Glavine, Mercker was feeling pain in his right side, an
injury that had bothered him occasionally ever since he aggravated the area swinging a bat in spring training several years
ago. He kept the injury quiet around reporters because he
didn't want to tip off opponents and remained hopeful the
pain would lessen with treatment. He had received two cortisone shots in the past two weeks, but the pain remained and
was affecting his pitching. He needed some time off, but refused to ask Cox to rest him. Each time the manager approached him and asked how he was feeling, Mercker said he
could pitch.

"I can't say no," he said. "It's killing me, but I can't say no."

Trainer Dave Pursley had examined Mercker and knew how much pain he was suffering. Before one game he advised Cox the reliever could use the day off, yet that night Mercker had been called into a game the Braves were losing 8–2 and had pitched two innings. Before each game Mercker would swallow several Advil and Excedrin to help deaden the pain, then head to the bullpen. Finally he decided he needed more cortisone to relieve the inflammation. Chandler gave him a double dose and added some Novocaine and steroids and it worked, at least for a while.

One of the reasons Mercker was willing to suffer the pain and the shots was that he was afraid Cox would leave him off the postseason roster if he complained. Last year's postseason had left a bad taste in his mouth. He had appeared in only one game in the playoffs, taking the loss in Game Four, and had pitched just one inning in the World Series. It rankled that Cox had turned to Mike Stanton as his primary left-handed reliever last October, and he wanted another shot at establishing himself as a pitcher the Braves could turn to in a big game. But the more he continued to pitch, the more he aggravated the injury. He wasn't pitching well, having allowed 16 earned runs in his last 15 innings, but he refused to take a week off and give his ribs a chance to recover. Chandler told him the pain could persist or it could clear up as quickly as it had arrived. He also warned him he might have to remove a rib if the injury continued to bother him. Finally, worried about the lingering pain and his ineffectiveness, the Braves sent Mercker to Piedmont Hospital, where Chandler performed a magnetic resonance imaging test. The test revealed a "hot spot" on his rib and Mercker reluctantly agreed to rest until the team returned from a road trip.

The Braves had been struck by the blahs. The offense wasn't clicking, the pitching was inconsistent, and they had lost three straight games. The Reds had trimmed their division lead to six and a half games, still a comfortable position, but the Braves were playing as if they felt comfortable. They were a team in need of a spark. Heading into the bottom of the ninth inning against the Phillies on a humid Saturday evening in Atlanta, the Braves were three outs away from a fourth consecutive loss. Ben Rivera, their old teammate, had limited them to five hits and a pair of runs, while the Phils had jumped on Avery for seven hits and five runs in six innings. Trailing by three runs in the ninth, Justice singled and Bream unloaded a home run, and Mitch Williams left the bullpen mound and sauntered into the game.

The left-hander had collected his twenty-third save the night before, preserving the 2–1 win in typical fashion: He had loaded the bases with no out in the ninth inning, then worked out of the jam, ending the game by forcing a double-play grounder from Berryhill. There was no such thing as a routine ninth inning with Williams—nicknamed "Wild Thing"—in a game. Lonnie Smith greeted him with a double and the crowd, sensing another dramatic ending, rose to its feet. Olson flied out, bringing Hunter to the plate as a pinch hitter, a role he felt uncomfortable in. One of the reasons he hated platooning with Bream was that he lost his confidence and rhythm at the plate with sporadic at-bats; pinch hitting was even worse. Usually he was sent to the plate to face a hard-throwing closer with the game on the line and was asked to produce a hit. Pinch hitting was one of baseball's toughest jobs, a role reserved for veteran players, and Hunter usually grumbled to himself when Cox sent him into the game.

Williams didn't pretend to know where any of his pitches were going—hence his nickname—and relied on a hair-raising fastball to intimidate and discourage hitters from digging in against him. He got ahead of Hunter 1-and-2 and decided on another fastball, which turned out to be his last pitch of the evening. Hunter was waiting on it and, like Pendleton three months before, he blasted it over the left field wall to give the Braves a 6–5 victory.

"Williams has confidence in his fastball and I have confidence I can hit one," Hunter said. "It was a good confrontation."

"I can't recall the last time we came back in the ninth inning, much less from four runs down," Olson remarked. "We were a couple of outs away from a manager's meeting and a team meeting."

Hunter's homer proved to be just the spark the Braves needed. It triggered a nine-game winning streak that for all intents and purposes put the pennant race to rest. Almost.


The frustration had begun to creep into Smoltz's voice and dominate his thoughts. He had won his fourteenth game back on August 6, matching his career-high total, and he secretly harbored hopes of catching Glavine and winning 20 games. His dreams had died during the dog days of August. He had held leads in several games and squandered them. In a couple of other starts the offense had sputtered. Smoltz had made five starts since gaining his fourteenth win and had come away empty each time. As he prepared to face the Dodgers on a rainy Labor Day afternoon in Atlanta, he told himself to relax and reviewed some of the mental exercises he and Jack Llewellyn had discussed. His relationship with the psychologist had remained strong, though he wasn't meeting with him as regularly as he once did. Smoltz felt he had matured and didn't need him as much as he had a year earlier. They played golf occasionally and Llewellyn still showed up for each of his starts dressed in the same bright red shirt and sat directly behind home plate where Smoltz could easily pick him out of the crowd. He still listened to the psychologist and appreciated his advice, but he bristled when he felt his talent was being overlooked and Llewellyn was being given too much credit for his development.

"It got to the point where it was like he won and he lost," Smoltz remarked.

He demonstrated his progress in dealing with adversity in

the first inning against the Dodgers. He didn't feel comfortable on the mound and opened the game by missing with his first 10 pitches, then made a nice recovery by striking out the next three hitters—Darryl Strawberry, Eric Karros, and Henry Rodriguez. He continued to miss with his fastball during the next few innings, but began snapping off his curve and mixing in an occasional forkball and picked up nine strikeouts in seven innings. The Braves gave him plenty of support, scoring three times in the fourth and three more times in the seventh, and Smoltz had a 7–1 victory. In the clubhouse afterward, relief flooded across his face and he smiled hugely as he lifted his shoulders in an exaggerated shrug.

"The monkey that was on my back should be running around here somewhere," he said. "It just seemed like I wanted to get my fifteenth win over with as quickly as I could and that probably prolonged it. To me it's a big lift and hopefully now I can relax the rest of the way."

Later, after the crowd had thinned in front of his locker, Smoltz leaned down and lifted up a bottle of champagne. He held it for a moment and a small satisfied smile tugged at the corners of his mouth.

"I'm not a champagne drinker," he said quietly, "but I will pop this tonight."


Glavine could feel the Cy Young Award slipping away from him. Hampered by the rib fracture that he still had not disclosed to most of his teammates, he had made three unsuccessful tries at his twentieth win. With it he had a good shot at repeating as the Cy Young winner; without it he didn't stand a chance. Cubs pitcher Greg Maddux was closing fast on his win total and held a better earned run average. More and more Glavine was hearing Maddux's name mentioned as the favorite for the Cy Young and he wondered how he had fallen out of favor in just a few weeks. It infuriated him to hear Peter Gammons report he was experiencing shoulder problems, another example of his substituting a lame rumor for fact, but he could not tell anyone the truth. Not yet. He would make another try for his twentieth and regardless of what happened he would maintain his ribs were sore, nothing more. However, as much as he tried to shove it out of his mind, Glavine knew there was much more at stake than a second straight 20-win season. His rib was not improving in the four days off between starts and he had to consider taking himself out of the rotation for a couple of weeks to recover if he was going to be ready to pitch in the playoffs. As he prepared to face the Reds in the first of two games in Atlanta, he knew the decision had to be made soon.

With his club in second place and trailing by seven and a half games, Piniella said the Reds had to win both games if they expected to catch the Braves. By the end of the first inning that hope was gone. The Braves scored seven runs in the first, three coming on Lonnie Smith's homer, and Glavine strode to the mound feeling his grasp begin to tighten on his twentieth win. It would not be easy. The fractured rib forced the left-hander to alter his delivery and caused a loss of accuracy with his pitches. He missed high and away repeatedly and when he attempted to adjust, his pitches flattened out. Virtually unarmed, he would make 87 pitches, missing with 40 of them, in five innings. The Reds scored a pair of runs in the second, then two more in the next two innings. Glavine survived the fourth, leaving the bases loaded, then swept through a perfect fifth, the first time he had retired the side in order. Cox decided enough was enough, he pulled Glavine, then held his breath the rest of the way as the Braves hung on for a 12–7 victory.

It was an ugly win, but Glavine was in no position to be choosy. He had his twentieth and decided he would take some time off to allow his rib to heal. Often during the next two weeks he would be quizzed about his chances for the Cy Young and be tempted to use his injury as an excuse for not winning his twentieth sooner.

Later he said, "If going out there and pitching hurt the last four weeks is going to hurt my chances for the Cy Young, then so be it. I won twenty games last year and it was good enough to win and I certainly feel it's good enough this year."

The Deion Sanders situation that had looked settled back in August was anything but. Although Sanders had assured the Braves he would be with them the remainder of the season, he had not given up hope of returning to the Falcons. It was a matter of money. Pay him enough and Sanders would hang-glide off the top of the Empire State Building. A story circulated that the first word Sanders taught to a parrot he had purchased for his daughter Deiondra was "money." He drove a four-wheel-drive truck with a front license plate that read "Deion $anders." If the Falcons wanted him, they would have to make him one of the NFL's best-paid defensive backs. The team had become increasingly desperate to get Sanders back into the secondary following a 366-yard passing performance by New York Jets quarterback Browning Nagle in the season opener, and Falcons president Taylor Smith stepped up talks with his agent, Eugene Parker. Brushing aside Sanders's accusation of a "plantation mentality," a charge he had leveled during negotiations the previous month, Smith piqued Parker's interest with a $2 million offer.

Sanders had maintained all along that his refusal to report to the team wasn't motivated by money, yet when the Falcons increased their offer Sanders prepared to flee the Braves. Two weeks before he had told TBS broadcaster Joe Simpson in an interview that the August negotiations with the Falcons "got beyond the point of money. It got to the point of principle. I have a dream of being a winner. Winning the World Series and the Super Bowl, and the World Series is going to come first."

Sanders would talk with Simpson and the other TBS broadcasters, but he refused to speak to reporters. He had begun refusing interviews following the publication of a column by *Atlanta Journal-Constitution* columnist Terence Moore in late August. In the column Moore had criticized Sanders for embarrassing himself by conducting negotiations with both the Falcons and Braves. He wrote, "There are a couple of things that Deion Sanders needs to do as soon as possible, and he can begin with this: He needs to shut up." Moore concluded by writing, "This business of Sanders trying to play pro football and pro baseball at the same time only will keep him from becoming the best that he can be at either sport. Somewhere it is written that man cannot serve two masters."

Sanders and Moore, who is also black, had feuded for several years. Moore had often taken Sanders to task for failing to provide what he considered a proper image for youngsters. Sanders had responded by becoming increasingly hostile toward Moore, and the pair had almost come to blows during a confrontation earlier in the season. After Moore's column appeared, Sanders blew up. He had told a writer earlier in the season that reporters should consider it a privilege to talk with him and he withdrew that privilege and refused to talk with anyone except his teammates.

"No one tells me to shut up," he had snapped.

Sanders decided to accept the Falcons' $2 million offer, a deal that would allow him to continue collecting his $1 million per year from Nike for playing both sports. He would split his time between the Falcons and Braves, a tradeoff that didn't completely satisfy either team, but one they were forced to accept. Sanders promised Schuerholz he would let Cox know when he would be available to play and indicated he would join the Braves exclusively during the postseason. Schuerholz didn't like the arrangement, fearing Sanders could suffer an injury with the Falcons and be lost for the playoffs, but he was powerless to prevent him from leaving.

"Everybody asks if playing two sports diminishes your skills to play both," he said. "The obvious answer is, sure it does."

Schuerholz had been through it all before with Bo Jackson in Kansas City, though Jackson had not reported to the Los Angeles Raiders until after the Royals' season was complete. He understood how unique the situation was, how unique Sanders was, a point driven home the same day Sanders reported to the Falcons. He practiced with the team in Suwanee, then hopped into his Toyota truck and sped south to the stadium in time to help the Braves complete a sweep of the Reds. He entered the game as a pinch runner in the bottom of the ninth inning with the score tied 2–2, forced an errant pickoff throw from pitcher Scott Bankhead, then raced home on Gant's sacrifice fly.

"It's only appropriate," Cox said. "He makes a deal with the Falcons, comes over here and scores the winning run and will probably score the winning TD Sunday against the Redskins. Just unbelievable."

In the clubhouse Olson watched Sanders plop a black hat on his head and brush past television crews and reporters without a word. While the Braves lingered, savoring their nine-and-a-half-game lead on the Reds, Sanders grabbed a duffel bag and headed for home.

"You guys might hate him," Olson said, watching the door close behind him, "but we love him."

Cox's prediction almost came true. The first time he touched the ball Sunday against the Redskins, Sanders scored a touchdown on a 99-yard kickoff return. Still, the Falcons lost 24–17.


After losing two games in Atlanta the previous week, Piniella had known the end was near. The Reds had stayed atop the West for nearly two months, even leading the Braves by four and a half games in mid-June, but injuries, a lack of production from the offense, and shoddy relief work by Charlton and Dibble had pushed them out of the race.

"I'm not conceding, but I'm realistic," Piniella had said.

He should have known it was not the Reds' year to win the West when first baseman Hal Morris injured his hamstring doing kneebends in the on-deck circle in Atlanta and was placed on the disabled list. If that didn't send a clear signal to him, certainly the sight of Glenn Braggs hobbling around the bases after straining his knee during a home run trot against the Braves, coupled with Roberts's neck injury, suffered after he slammed into the center field wall, should have been enough. Piniella was left shaking his head and bemoaning the team's fate.

"We've had a few things happen that I've never seen before," he said. "When I go to sleep at night, I think I'm hallucinating."

When the Braves arrived in Cincinnati for a three-game series, the deficit was 10½ games and even the most optimistic voice in the home clubhouse couldn't muster any hope of catching them.

"I didn't think any one team would run away with this," Reds second baseman Bill Doran said sadly.

Before the series opened, the Braves gathered at The Waterfront, a well-known restaurant perched on the banks of the Ohio River, for their team party, an annual bash paid for from the fines collected in kangaroo court. Justice, a Cincinnati native, was in charge and weeks earlier he had arranged for everyone to draw the name of a teammate from a hat and buy a gag gift. Pendleton received a cane. Yost was given a paint-by-numbers set. Belliard received a "Million Dollar Man" doll. When all the gifts had been handed out, Nixon was left empty-handed. Justice had forgotten to put his name in the hat.

Blauser had to laugh because he knew how Nixon felt. He had suffered more than his share of indignities in the last few years and felt he had often been overlooked. He still remembered the foulup last year that had prevented him from being named the league's Player of the Week, an award that recognized the player with the best offensive statistics each week. Blauser had never won it before, but after hitting three homers and driving in 13 runs, he figured he was an easy choice. However, the team's public relations department forgot to nominate him to the league office and he had not won. Blauser didn't say anything, but he was deeply hurt and the incident reinforced his feelings that he was viewed as a backup player and didn't belong in the same company as Pendleton and Justice and the others. It was an attitude he was slowly changing. He was finally playing regularly as Cox's confidence in him grew, and much to everyone's surprise he had become a solid, sure-handed shortstop. Aside from a shaky start to his pro career, he had always been regarded as a good hitter. Blauser could look back at his first season in the minor leagues and chuckle, but for a while he thought he might be released. He had been banished to the backwaters of Virginia, assigned to the Rookie League Pulaski team, and had begun his career by going hitless in his first 33 at-bats.

"I called my mom and told her I didn't think I'd be there for long," he recalled. "When I finally got my first hit, even though it was an error, everybody in the dugout stood up and clapped."

Cox was now hitting him in the number two slot in the order, following Nixon and ahead of Pendleton. Even as he was proving himself as a regular, Blauser remained the club's Rodney Dangerfield, unable to draw respect from any quarter. Like most players, he had a deal with a shoe company to be supplied with spikes and other footwear in return for his endorsement. However, every time he ordered a new pair of spikes from Nike, they sent him the wrong size. He had become impatient and was ready to change companies, but he put in one last order and was delighted when a box was delivered several days later. He eagerly tore it open, only to discover Nike had sent along a pair of Dodger-blue spikes. He figured that best exemplified the respect he was accorded, and he retaliated by wearing a pair of Reeboks. The latest indignity involved his garment bag. Blauser had reported it missing when it wasn't delivered to his hotel room in Houston, but figured a teammate was playing a prank on him and didn't begin to worry until he reached Cincinnati and it still had not appeared. He had $2,000 worth of clothes in the bag, yet it had failed to turn up after a search of the truck carrying the team's luggage and equipment. Blauser's bag was the only one missing and after he returned home he discussed the loss with the club's Delta representative, but it was never found.

Blauser would persevere. While he was in Cincinnati, he learned he had been named the league's Player of the Week after hitting .545 with three RBIs.

"I was going to go up to him and say, 'Sorry, Jeff, we forgot to nominate you,' but I just congratulated him," joked Jim Schultz, the club's public relations director.

The Reds beat Avery 4–2 in the first game of the series, though the left-hander gave up just five hits and three runs in seven innings. It was a perfect example of the way Avery's season had gone. He had become the designated fall guy for the club's offense. He could pitch in the middle of a hot streak by the hitters and they would score only a run or two while he was on the mound, then he would watch from the dugout the next day as Glavine or Smoltz received six or seven runs. It was especially annoying to him because he felt he was pitching better than he had the previous season, yet he couldn't push his won-lost record past .500.

"A couple of runs here, a couple of runs there, and Steve has fifteen or sixteen wins," Olson offered.

The magic Avery had displayed in last October's playoffs had not materialized again. He had been named the series MVP after beating the Pirates twice, though the Braves had managed just one run in each game, and that same level of offense had shadowed him all season. While the Braves had won his last three starts, they had done so in the final inning, long after he had been pulled for a pinch hitter. They had ridden into Riverfront Stadium on a nine-game winning streak and were averaging more than seven runs per game, but had managed to score just two when Avery was around. That was the kind of luck he had experienced.

"It just seems there are some games I'm not meant to win," he said.

The Braves won the second game 3–2, but dropped the series finale by the same score. Later, they were amused to hear of a rumble in the Reds clubhouse following the game.

Piniella had used rookie pitcher Steve Foster to close the game, explaining later that Dibble had told him his shoulder felt tight and he couldn't pitch. Not true, Dibble charged, describing his manager as "a liar." Reporters carried that message back to Piniella, who became infuriated, rushed from his office, and grabbed Dibble. The pair traded punches before several players rushed in and pulled them apart with Piniella emerging, in the words of a Cincinnati writer, "clearly the winner."

Greg Olson's season ended with a jarring crash, a home plate collision that would remain freeze-framed in his mind's eye forever. In the opener of a brief homestand against the Astros, he was standing at home plate awaiting a throw from Justice when Ken Caminiti lowered his shoulder and plowed into him.

"You have a sense of when it might be collision time," he said later. "But I don't think I've ever been hit that hard."

Caminiti, attempting to score from third base on Pete Incaviglia's fly, arrived at the plate an instant behind the ball. A stocky, muscular third baseman, he had only average speed, and Cox admitted later he was surprised to see him attempt to score on the shallow fly. As Caminiti bore down on Olson, Bream gloved Justice's throw, whirled, and relayed the ball to the plate. Taking the throw from his right, Olson was blind to the runner. He half-turned, met Caminiti's charge, and was somersaulted backward by the impact.

"If he'd given me a little bit of the plate I probably would have tried to slide," Caminiti remarked afterward.

In a scene eerily reminiscent of his head-stand somersault in Game One of the 1991 World Series, Olson hung on to the ball and flopped over on his stomach, dazed and badly shaken.

"The play is a catcher's nightmare," he said afterward. "You really don't know what's coming. You have about an eighth of a second and you get smoked."

Pain knifed through his right ankle, and as assistant trainer Jeff Porter reached him, Olson turned and looked at his leg.

"Just tell me it's a bad sprain," he told Porter.

Porter, who acknowledged later he knew immediately that Olson's ankle was badly damaged, looked him in the eye and offered, "I can't tell right now, but you never know, it might be."

Olson knew he was lying.

"My cleat got caught and as soon as I went over I knew something was wrong," he said. "Before I even hit the ground I felt a warm, burning sensation in my leg."

Olson had suffered a fractured ankle involving two torn ligaments, as well as a broken fibula. As his anxious team-mates clustered around home plate, Porter fixed an inflatable cast to Olson's ankle and strapped a brace around his neck. The realization that his season was over wouldn't hit Olson until later. As he was loaded onto a cart, he remembered that his wife, Lisa, would be watching on television and worrying about him. As the hushed crowd began to cheer, he lifted his arm and began a tomahawk chop. Watching from the visitors' dugout, Caminiti felt a pang of guilt.

"Thinking about him being out for the season really gets me," he said. "I mean, they're going to be in the playoffs and our season is going to be over. It doesn't seem fair."

Doctors didn't waste any time in repairing Olson's ankle. A few hours after the game ended he was wheeled into an operating room at Piedmont Hospital and during an hour-long procedure a screw was inserted in his ankle and a cast molded to his leg. The next day his room would be awash in flowers, balloons, and candy sent by fans.

The loss of Olson caused Cox to gulp nervously. Berryhill would become the regular catcher and be backed up by a rookie, Javier Lopez, who had made his major league debut several innings after Olson was injured and had no experience above Class AA ball. It was a tenuous arrangement. Berryhill had more power at the plate than Olson, but he could not match his defensive skills or his relationship with the pitchers.

Despite the ribbing Olson received for refusing to turn down gift offers or appearance money, he was a popular teammate and called a good game. Corrales had called him the best catcher he had ever seen at blocking balls in the dirt, a skill that translated into increased confidence for pitchers, who weren't afraid to bounce a pitch at the plate.

"Emotionally, it's a pretty big blow," Blauser said. "Losing a guy of his defensive capabilities is going to be tough."

Berryhill was an adequate receiver, but he didn't have quite the rapport with the pitchers that Olson did. But that was not what bothered Cox. He felt uncomfortable with having one experienced catcher on hand for the playoffs, but with no other catcher available in the minor leagues, he was stuck with Lopez. If Berryhill got injured, the Braves would be in trouble.

"I'm not worried about getting hurt," he said. "If there's a play at the plate I'll make the play. I'm not going to change a thing. To me, there's no pressure."


The Braves hoped to clinch the division on a seven-game swing to the West Coast in the next-to-last week of the season. Their magic number stood at seven and the sooner they could wrap up the title, the sooner Pendleton and the other regulars could take a break. The trip began promisingly as Pete Smith took a 4–2 win in Dodger Stadium, but Smoltz lost the next day and the Reds pushed their win streak to six games by sweeping a doubleheader from the Astros. The Braves moved north next and ganged up on Bud Black in San Francisco as Leibrandt beat his former Kansas City teammate 7–0. Then the offense vanished. Glavine was a 4–0 loser to the Giants, and Avery's hard-luck season continued in San Diego, where he took a 1–0 loss. Suddenly, the Reds, now riding a nine-game win streak, had crept to within four and a half games and the Braves glanced nervously in their rear-view mirror.

"We've just got to get back that same cockiness we had a couple of months ago when we went out on the field knowing that we were going to win," Glavine fretted.

Just as they had done last year, the Giants arrived in the nick of time to help the Braves. They had eliminated the Dodgers on the next-to-last day last season, and this time they halted Cincinnati's win streak during a Saturday afternoon game at Candlestick. It would take the Braves 10 innings, but they would beat the Padres 2–1 later that night, then wrap up the trip with another 2–1 victory the next afternoon. Hunter tied the game in the ninth with a two-out double and Pendleton drove in the winning run with another two-out hit the next inning. The magic number was down to two and the relief was evident in the Braves clubhouse.

"When we had that ten-and-a-half-game lead, I really think it made us relax more than we should have," Pendleton said. "I know I found myself relaxing. But we turned around forward the last two days and now we can clinch it at home."

As the team's charter climbed above San Diego and turned east, Cox considered the fast-approaching playoffs and worried about the bullpen. Although Reardon and Stanton had pitched well on the trip, he was concerned about the depth behind them. Pena remained out with tendinitis in his elbow and Mercker was sitting at home resting his ribs. Wohlers had done a good job since being recalled from Richmond at the end of August, but he didn't like shifting the responsibility and pressure of the playoffs onto a rookie's shoulders. He could use Freeman and keep his fingers crossed; the right-hander was pitching well, but he could fall into a rut as quickly as any pitcher he had ever seen. If his hard sinker was working, then he was fine. If it wasn't, he didn't have any other weapons and usually got pounded.

Cox reached several decisions. He chose to abandon the four-man rotation he had used in last October's playoffs and go with three starting pitchers. He would shift Pete Smith and Leibrandt to the bullpen, which would give him an extra left-hander in case Mercker could not pitch, but it would also place a burden on the starting trio of Smoltz, Avery, and Glavine. Leibrandt's face fell when he was told of Cox's decision.

"Of course I'm disappointed," he said. "I'd love to be out

there starting, but they make the decisions and I follow orders."

The scoreboard kept updating the Reds-Dodgers game in Cincinnati, and each time Los Angeles scored a roar rose from the crowd at Atlanta–Fulton County Stadium. It seemed appropriate that Leibrandt was on the mound, facing Black and the Giants for the second time in six days, because he wasn't certain he would get another chance to pitch this season. It was a mild Tuesday evening and Leibrandt knew a win, coupled with a Reds loss, would clinch the division. He had been on four division championship teams during his career, but he had never pitched a clinching game and he wanted very badly to experience the same exhilaration that Smoltz had in pitching the deciding game last October. The Giants picked up two hits in the second inning and another pair in the third, but Leibrandt bore down each time and stranded the runners. Gant gave him a 1–0 lead with a homer in the second, then the Braves scored four times in the fourth and they shifted their attention to the scoreboard, where the Dodgers continued to lead the Reds. Leibrandt maintained his focus, yielding two more hits in the fifth and another in the sixth, but no Giant crossed home plate. He had completed a perfect eighth inning and was in the dugout when a resounding roar shook the stadium. It was all over at Riverfront Stadium, where the Dodgers beat the Reds 5–0. The Braves needed just three outs to win the West.

Leibrandt got the first two outs in the ninth and faced pinch hitter John Patterson. In center field Nixon, whose suspension had cost him any role in the season-end celebrations last year, silently pleaded for the final out to head in his direction.

"I was saying, 'God, let me get this ball, let it come to me,' " he said later. "David [Justice] was saying the same thing. He wanted it too. But I don't think anybody in the stadium wanted it more than I did."

Leibrandt made his pitch and Patterson lifted a fly toward

Nixon. Glancing over his shoulder, Leibrandt saw the center fielder camped beneath it and he ran toward Berryhill and hugged him as the Braves poured from the dugout. In center, Nixon raised his arms in triumph and offered a soft thank-you toward the heavens.

"I don't think anybody last year would have said, 'Next year Otis Nixon is going to get the last out, that he's going to grab the ball and hang on to it,' " he said later. "But that's what I did. I'm going to cherish this forever."

The Braves ran up the tunnel and into the clubhouse and a few minutes later they reappeared on the field wearing T-shirts enscribed with "National League West Champions." They jogged around the warning track waving and shouting, enjoying the sweet sound of raucous, foot-stomping adulation.

"Everybody said we couldn't do it again and we did," Olson shouted afterward over the din in the clubhouse. "This winning in front of the home crowd really stirs up the heartbeat."

The clubhouse was draped in plastic as champagne spurted everywhere. Schuerholz stood off to one side watching quietly, a satisfied smile on his face.

"It's very difficult to repeat," he said. "To do it is a reflection of the ability and character of this ballclub."

Last October the celebration had been spontaneous and uproarious. This time it was more like a fraternity house party. The Braves toasted their success and congratulated themselves, but unlike last year when the approaching playoffs had seemed like a great adventure, the pressure of the looming postseason was already being felt.

"You won't see a lot of rah-rah from this team until we get back to the World Series," Glavine noted.

This year, stopping one run shy of the championship would not feel like enough.

# THE PLAYOFFS

Drums were pounding along Capitol Avenue. These weren't the small drums carried in high school marching bands, but deep-throated kettledrums whose booming tones could be heard from blocks away. Fans had been gathering all afternoon outside Atlanta–Fulton County Stadium, and now they stood three deep at an entrance, waving and cheering as each player drove up and disappeared into the tunnel leading to the clubhouse. It had been a week since the Braves clinched the division championship, and five hours before they would open the National League Championship Series against the Pittsburgh Pirates a festival had sprung up outside the stadium. Balloons, flags, and pennants fluttered in the breeze, vendors hawking T-shirts and foam rubber tomahawks prowled the grounds, and people holding signs that read "Need a Ticket!" lined the sidewalk and peered, their faces hopeful, into slow-moving cars.

It was largely the same atmosphere that gripped Atlanta last October, though some of the frenzied excitement was missing. As one fan remarked outside the stadium, "Last year, it was like a wide-eyed Christmas morning. I was in awe of the team. Now, we're just proud." The Braves felt much the same way; they had lost their innocence marching to the World Series last year, and now the weight of great expectations rested heavily on their shoulders.

"It will be tougher because we expect more ourselves," Glavine said. "If we don't win the World Series we'll be disappointed. There's some pressure in that sense."

While 1991 was magical for the Braves, in many ways this season had been more satisfying. They had set out in April to accomplish something no National League West team had done since the 1977–78 Dodgers: win consecutive division titles. Despite last year's success, many experts picked them to finish behind the Reds, and that seemed all too accurate in late May when the Braves tumbled into last place, seven games under .500. Then came their remarkable resurgence, which included a record-tying 13-game winning streak, a three-month roll that carried them to the top of the West with the major leagues' best record.

"I expected us to play the way we have," Pendleton said. "Last year I expected it too, but no one else did."

Even in the lowest days of May, when nothing seemed to go right, and both pitching and offense were nowhere to be found, the Braves didn't lose their focus. Despite the many players grumbling about their lack of playing time and others longing to be traded, they had collected the most wins in baseball, a franchise record 98. As they prepared to meet the Pirates in Game One, Glavine reflected everyone's thoughts: "I'm looking forward to going out and getting a bigger and better ring."

Cox had chosen Smoltz to start the first game against the Pirates, with Avery and Glavine to follow. His decision reflected his confidence in Smoltz, and his uncertainty about Glavine's rib injury. If the series went seven games Smoltz would start three times, while Glavine and Avery would pitch twice each. The last time Smoltz had faced Pittsburgh in the playoffs, he pitched a shutout in Game Seven last October, and he was eager to be the focal point again.

"If you try and treat it any differently from any other game, you put extra pressure on yourself," he said. "Any playoff game is a pressure start, but somebody's got to start and I'm glad it's me."

Greg Olson was a born ham, and even on crutches, unable to play in the series, he managed to be the center of attention before Game One. He had asked his mother-in-law to paint a tomahawk on his cast and he showed it off to the hundreds of reporters and camera crews gathered around the batting cage. Olson planned to have all the Braves sign the cast, then it would be auctioned off to benefit the American SIDS (Sudden Infant Death Syndrome) Institute.

"It looked a little drab," he explained. "It's going to be a little smelly when it finally comes off, but maybe we can make a lot of money from it. There are so many bad aspects to this cast—I can't play, I can't drive, I can't hunt—but at least one good thing can come from it."

The Braves were creatures of habit and they kept to their usual routine before the playoff games. Olson, Leibrandt, and Smoltz sat at a table in the clubhouse playing cards, while Bream answered mail, and Avery and other players played a Skins putting game, using drainage openings in the carpeted floor as holes. An hour before batting practice started, Cox called a meeting to discuss the scouting report on the Pirates. Mazzone went over Pittsburgh's hitters, pointing out their strengths and weaknesses, then third base coach Jimy Williams set the defensive alignment for each hitter. It wasn't a long meeting; the two teams were thoroughly familiar with each other, having met 12 times during the season. Still, the scouting reports were important. The Braves had won 7 of the 12 games against the Pirates, and Cox credited advance scout Bobby Wine's reports with helping Atlanta's pitchers shut down Pittsburgh's three and four hitters, Andy Van Slyke and Bobby Bonds.

Smoltz hid his nervousness behind a wide smile and laughter during batting practice. Like Glavine, he felt jumpy before every start, but his jitters usually lasted only a pitch or two. Smoltz knew it was important for him to pitch well to boost both his own confidence and that of his teammates. Jack Llewellyn approached him and they chatted for a few minutes. His relationship with the psychologist had changed during the last few months. As his confidence increased, Smoltz had weaned himself away from Llewellyn, and they began acting as friends instead of as doctor and patient. Bothered off and on by a sore groin during the final two months, Smoltz had again finished the season feeling disappointed. He had won only one game after August 6 and his dream of matching Glavine's 20-win season had faded away. The playoffs offered him a chance to redeem himself, and he relished facing the Pirates again after beating them twice in last October's postseason.

"As a kid, I was always pretending to be in situations where I'd be pitching the big game," Smoltz said. "I enjoy being given the opportunity to pitch in games like this."

A wintry breeze rippled the flag in center field as he headed to the mound. His plan was to establish his fastball early in the game, then rely on his slider and forkball later when the Pirates were expecting the fastball. He felt comfortable and confident, and he roared through four innings without allowing a hit. Meanwhile, the Braves jumped on Pirates starter Doug Drabek with a run in the second inning when Lemke singled home Bream, then pushed two more runs across in the fourth.

Pittsburgh second baseman Jose Lind broke up Smoltz's no-hitter with a two-out single in the fifth, then hit a solo homer in the eighth, but by that time it was too late: The Braves led 5-0 and they would win by the same 5–1 score that the Pirates used to win Game One last October. Smoltz had simply overpowered Pittsburgh. He had collected six strikeouts in eight innings, and had limited Van Slyke and Bonds to one single in five at-bats.

"I gained a lot from last year," Smoltz said afterwards.

"Game Seven of the World Series was the ultimate game. Compared to that, tonight was a piece of cake."

Although he had played in few games with the Braves since deciding to rejoin the Falcons in September, and did not play in Game One against the Pirates, Deion Sanders still managed to attract attention. He had made it known he might try to play two sports in one day; for the Falcons against the Dolphins in Miami on Sunday afternoon, then for the Braves in Pittsburgh that night, if the series lasted five games. His plan angered Schuerholz, who felt Sanders was going back on his word that he would play exclusively for the Braves during the postseason.

"We were told he would be full time with us," Schuerholz tersely told a group of reporters. "A lot of people make a big deal about this guy. I'm not. No individual is more important than this team. This team has worked too hard to get here, and nothing is going to get in the way of that."

Although Sanders had not informed Cox or Schuerholz of his plans, he had already made up his mind he would play for the Falcons on Sunday. He planned to charter a jet and fly to Florida following Game Four in Pittsburgh on Saturday night, then hop the plane back in time to be in the dugout for the start of Game Five. There were several reasons why Sanders decided to play both sports in one day, not the least of which involved money. He stood to lose $118,000 in pay from the Falcons if he missed the game. Also, Nike planned to use footage of his odyssey for a new commercial.

Sanders continued to ignore the media, so reporters dogged Schuerholz's footsteps. Would Deion play for the Falcons? Didn't he agree to play solely for the Braves during the postseason? Schuerholz maintained that Sanders had promised to play exclusively for the Braves, and he was plainly unhappy at having to field questions about the situation. Later, Sanders would claim the general manager misunderstood the agreement. "Nobody said we couldn't play football," Sanders said.

"We gave our word we'd play baseball full time, and that's what I did."

(A week after the incident, Sanders broke his silence with the media long enough to charge in an interview with *New York Newsday* that Schuerholz had started a public campaign against him by talking to reporters about his situation.

"It hurts," he said. "I don't like Schuerholz trying to damage my credibility. One thing I pride myself on is being real. If a man ain't got his word, he ain't got nothing.")

Schuerholz was annoyed by Sanders's bluster. He responded by saying, "There are some people I've known in my life that I respect, and I'd be hurt if they were critical of me. He's not one of them."


Ron Gant remained frustrated by the decline of his offensive skills. He had been an MVP candidate in 1991, but now he was no factor in the Braves lineup. His power had vanished and he continued flailing away at the plate. Cox kept him in the lineup, hoping he would regain his stroke in time for the playoffs, but he had also played Lonnie Smith during the final weeks of the season in case he decided to replace Gant. At last, Cox's patience was rewarded; as the season wound down he caught glimpses of Gant's old powerful swing. Gant had hit .407 with three homers in his last eight games, and appeared comfortable at the plate again. But he had been hitless in Game One and struck out twice, and Cox wondered if he had fallen back into his bad habits. Nonetheless, he wrote Gant's name onto the lineup card, hitting sixth, and crossed his fingers.

Avery would start Game Two, and he held a psychological edge on the Pirates. He had faced them twice in last year's playoffs, establishing an LCS record by pitching 16⅓ shutout innings, then being named the series MVP after winning both games by 1–0 scores. But like Smoltz, he was disappointed in how this season had ended. He had finished with an 11–11 record, seven fewer wins than he had in 1991, and had won just once since the middle of August. Although he knew his record really wasn't an accurate reflection of his pitching— the Braves scored two runs or fewer in six of his losses—he still felt dissatisfied. Pitching well in the playoffs would ease his disappointment.

Avery carried those thoughts to the mound on the afternoon of October 7, little more than 15 hours after Game One had ended. Pirates manager Jim Leyland had made two changes in his lineup, adding a pair of right-handed hitters— first baseman Gary Redus and right fielder Lloyd McClendon —against the left-hander, but Avery's focus remained on Van Slyke and Bonds. If he could match Smoltz's success against the duo, he felt confident he would win.

Following Smoltz's example, he roared through the Pirates, allowing just two hits in six innings. He had yanked his cap down low on his forehead, so that when a hitter stared out at the mound, all he could see of his eyes was a menacing, shadowed glint; the effect was like peering into a cave entrance and spotting a set of glowing yellow orbs. Sitting on the bench, his eyes fixed on Avery, Mazzone smiled to himself when he saw him yank on his cap.

"That means he's ready to roll, he's locked in," Mazzone said later. "I told him coming down the wire that he should pull it down even lower."

Leyland had decided to start left-hander Danny Jackson against the Braves, though all the statistics suggested that wasn't a wise choice. Jackson made six starts against the Braves during the season, and emerged with an 0–4 record and a 4.19 earned run average. Four of those starts came while he was pitching for the Cubs, but it didn't seem to matter what uniform he wore when he faced the Braves— they loved to see him. Jackson, who had pitched in both leagues and was a 10-year veteran, had not beaten the Braves in Atlanta in more than four years.

He would not last two innings. The Braves led 4–0 before he was mercifully removed, and former Brave Bob Walk replaced him. The hit parade continued. Gant reached the plate with the bases loaded in the fifth and sent a pitch climbing toward the Goodyear blimp, which was circling beyond the left field stands. Walk's head swiveled to follow the flight of the ball, his face grew long and his shoulders slumped. Trotting down the first base line, Gant pumped his fist excitedly, then motioned toward family and friends in the stands as he crossed home plate.

"I can't remember what was going through my mind, but I know I was excited," he would say later.

Gant's grand slam, the fourth in NLCS history, gave the Braves an 8–0 lead and capped an explosive afternoon. They collected 14 hits and accepted 8 walks from seven Pirates pitchers in a 13–5 victory. Besides Gant's two hits and four RBIs, Pendleton had a pair of hits and drove in two runs, Lemke collected three hits, and Justice reached base three times and drove in a pair of runs. Avery's concentration wavered in the seventh and he yielded four runs, snapping his playoff-record shutout streak at 22⅓ innings, but it hardly mattered. The Braves led the best-of-seven series two games to none and the Pirates were deflated and reeling.

"We've been getting our heads beat in and we've got a headache," Van Slyke said. "We're in the emergency room and we hope we're not in intensive care by Friday."


Bruce Dal Canton has an easy smile and a mean knuckleball. A former pitcher with four major league teams, he had been the Braves pitching coach for four years when Cox took over as manager and demoted him to Richmond. Dal Canton, a gray-haired, soft-spoken man, had accepted the move with grace, though the success of the Braves pitching staff during the next two years surely gnawed at him; Mazzone had been promoted from Richmond to replace him and inherited a staff ready to blossom.

Now the Braves needed Dal Canton. Schuerholz and Cox had decided the best way to prepare for Pirates knuckleball pitcher Tim Wakefield, scheduled to start Game Three, was to swing at knuckleballs. With the series shifting to Three Rivers Stadium, Dal Canton agreed to leave his home outside Pittsburgh and throw knuckleballs during batting practice. Cox's reasoning was sound: The more knuckleballs the Braves saw, he figured, the better they would adjust to Wakefield. However, the flaw in his strategy soon became evident. Even as he attempted to let the Braves hit his pitches, Dal Canton's knuckleballs were aggravating. They hit few of his pitches solidly, which didn't lessen their confidence, but did nothing to strengthen it either. Facing a knuckleball pitcher isn't like preparing to face a pitcher throwing a wicked curve or one using a forkball as his primary pitch. A knuckleball has a mind of its own. Once Wakefield releases it, he has no idea where it will go or what it will do. It could dip, dart, tumble, or swerve. It could hit catcher Don Slaught on the mask or slide past him and hit the backstop.

"I'd rather face a guy who throws a hundred miles an hour than one of those guys," Ted Williams once said of a knuckleballer. "If the pitcher doesn't know where it's going, how in the hell am I supposed to know?"

The beauty of the pitch, and its curse, is that few pitchers throw it because of the difficulty of controlling it. Hitters see few knuckleballs during a season, which only increases their difficulty in hitting them. All in all, Wakefield had a sizable advantage.

"You just hope Wakefield doesn't have his best knuckleball on Friday," Justice said, shrugging. "If he does, it's going to be extremely tough."

Wakefield had tantalized the Braves with his fluttering pitch in August and emerged with a 4–2 win in Pittsburgh. A former first baseman, the 26-year-old rookie had turned to the knuckleball as a means of salvaging his career and had became the Pirates savior. He stood the National League on its ear, winning eight of nine decisions after being recalled from the minors in July. Flailing away at Wakefield's knuckleball two months before, an exercise that had brought them only seven hits, the Braves had shaken their heads ruefully and tipped their caps to the youngster.

"It's like a butterfly coming toward you," Nixon said. "They don't fly straight. They fly all over the place. That's what you see with a knuckleball."

Offered Bream, "Can you imagine being on a trampoline and catching a ball while jumping up and down? With a good knuckleball, that's what it's like."

The Braves would counter with Glavine, who insisted his rib was fully healed. He had some unpleasant playoff memories to motivate him. Though he had pitched well last year, he had lost both his starts against the Pirates in the championship series, and he felt he had something to prove. He took that attitude to the mound and Redus, the first hitter he faced, promptly sent a drive up the right center field gap and dashed around the bases with a triple. Glavine's face remained impassive. He rarely displayed emotion on the field, and as Jay Bell, the Pirates shortstop, settled in at the plate, he stared off into space and chewed thoughtfully on his gum. Glavine got Bell on a comeback grounder to the mound. Then he forced a grounder from Van Slyke, and got another ground ball from Bonds to strand Redus at third. Striding from the mound, Glavine stepped out of character for a moment. His stern expression dissolved and he pumped his fist excitedly.

But the Braves discovered Wakefield was as unflappable as Glavine. They put runners on first and second with no outs in the second, then threatened him again by putting another pair on the next inning, and couldn't score either time. Wakefield survived each jam by getting a double-play grounder, first from Gant, then from Blauser. His knuckleballs hung in the crisp air like snowflakes, but seemed to melt just as they reached the plate.

"The knuckleball comes in looking like a basketball, but when you swing it looks like a golf ball," Pendleton said later.

Wakefield stayed with his knuckleball, later estimating that 90 percent of his 109 pitches were knucklers; only two failed to approach the plate tracing an erratic path. Bream clubbed a home run in the fourth and Gant hit another in the seventh, but the damage was minimal. Both were solo shots.

Glavine's first inning set the tone for the evening. He wandered in and out of trouble, but didn't give up a run until the fifth, when Slaught yanked a high changeup over the left field wall. Glavine knew the remaining four innings would be a struggle. His pitches lacked their usual crispness and his control was spotty. He gave up another run in the sixth when Van Slyke opened with a double and Jeff King slammed another two-base hit. With the score tied 2–2 in the seventh, Redus singled with one out and Bell followed with a double. Cox decided he had seen enough. With Van Slyke and Bonds next, he walked slowly to the mound and signaled for Stanton. It wasn't a tough decision: One of Cox's favorite strategies is to match Stanton against the league's best left-handed hitters. Even as Stanton had struggled through the first half, Cox had gone to him frequently and he had finally shown signs of regaining his dominance in August. Mercker had had that brief weekend of glory against the Reds in June, but had disappeared as Stanton emerged as Cox's number one left-hander out of the bullpen.

In Van Slyke and Bonds, Stanton faced a pair of hitters who were feeling pressure to produce some offense. Bonds in particular had picked up a reputation as a player who choked in the postseason after hitting .167 and .148 in the 1990 and 1991 playoffs, while Van Slyke approached the plate with just 2 hits in 12 at-bats in the series.

"It seems like the weight of the world is on their shoulders and they probably feel like they have to carry the whole team," Avery had said after Game Two.

Stanton got ahead of Van Slyke 1-and-2 with two fastballs and a curve, then he wasted a pitch. His next pitch was a fastball and Van Slyke swung and lifted a medium-depth fly to Justice in right. Redus retreated to third, and as the ball settled into Justice's glove he tagged up and sprinted home with the go-ahead run.

That would be enough for Wakefield. Nixon gave him an anxious moment in the eighth with a two-out double, but he retired Blauser on a grounder, then got Pendleton, Justice, and Bream in the ninth. A huge smile plastered on his face, Wakefield walked from the field into the smothering embrace of his teammates.

"It's exciting to finally have a dream come true," he said. "A rookie winning a game in the championship series. This is very special to me."

Otis Nixon had lived with the ache in his heart for a year. He would never forget his ordeal inside a drug treatment center the previous fall, a painful reawakening made far worse as he watched the Braves beat the Pirates in the playoffs and advance to the World Series. He had sat in front of a television and watched with a smile as his teammates celebrated in Pittsburgh, then wiped away the tears after the Game Seven loss in Minnesota.

"I was going through a lot of pain [at the center] and dealing with a lot of things I had to deal with regardless of whether I was going to play baseball or do anything else in life," Nixon recalled. "For me to go through that and not be there with my teammates, that was hard."

No one wanted the Braves to return to the playoffs more than Nixon. It saddened him that he had let his teammates down, and the only way to make it up to them was if they repeated as champions together. As the Braves took batting practice before Game Four on another chilly night at Three Rivers Stadium, Nixon was feeling relaxed and confident. He had reached base six times in 15 plate appearances in the first three games and scored three runs. It was time to show what he could really do.

The starting pitchers in Game One, Smoltz and Drabek, would head to the mound for a rematch. Only the advantage of modern sports medicine allowed Smoltz to work again so quickly. He had suffered an upper back strain in Game One and the next day he was barely able to get out of bed. Working quietly so the Pirates wouldn't learn of the injury, trainers gave him a cortisone shot to relieve the inflammation, a chiropractor manipulated his back, and then he was treated with electrical stimulation and whirlpools. By the time he reached the mound to face the Pirates, he felt almost as good as new.

Still, he was tentative in his approach as he subconsciously waited for the pain to reappear, and he had a rough three innings. His pitches weren't sharp and he gave up a pair of runs in the second and another run the next inning before he finally began to feel comfortable. He sped through the middle innings, retiring nine straight hitters, and reached the seventh with a three-run lead. However, Alex Cole walked and Van Slyke doubled him home, and Cox shuffled from the dugout and made his way to the mound. He had Stanton ready in the bullpen with Bonds at the plate, and he decided to make the change. Bonds, who had just one hit in the series, went down swinging, and King bounced out to Lemke at second, stranding Van Slyke at second base.

Like Smoltz, Drabek wasn't sharp early. Nixon had opened the game with a single, then stole second, but Blauser, Pendleton, and Justice were unable to drive him home. The next inning he arrived at the plate with two out and Lemke and Smoltz on base, and singled again, driving in Lemke. Atlanta trailed 3–2 in the fifth inning when Nixon led off with his third hit. A sense of confidence began to build in the Braves dugout. Blauser singled and one out later Justice came to the plate with Nixon, representing the tying run, standing on third base.

"I swear, I was standing on first thinking, 'Justice is made for this moment,'" Blauser would say later. "I was thinking he is going to hit a line drive, and I just don't want it to hit me."

Justice made Blauser seem a prophet. After fouling off nine pitches, he drove a Drabek offering into right field for a hit and Leyland hurried to the mound to rescue his beleaguered right-hander. He called in lefty Randy Tomlin; Cox countered by sending Hunter to the plate to pinch hit for Bream. It was a move Cox had made throughout the season, though Hunter remained one of the club's worst pinch hitters with a .239 batting average. He never felt comfortable coming off the bench cold, and his frequent pinch-hitting appearances had contributed to his deteriorating relationship with Cox. He approached the plate against Tomlin, a sidearm pitcher with sweeping breaking pitches, needing only to lift a fly to the outfield to score Blauser with the go-ahead run. Instead, he chopped a high bouncer to King at third, but King's hurried throw home pulled catcher Mike LaValliere away from the plate, and Blauser scooted in just ahead of the tag for a 4–3 lead.

The Braves pressed their advantage the next inning. Smoltz singled with two out, and when Tomlin and first baseman Orlando Merced paid no attention to him he stole second. It was an unpardonable gaffe by the Pirates to allow Smoltz to move into scoring position with Nixon at the plate. Leyland was left shaking his head in the dugout when Nixon heaped on the embarrassment by driving in Smoltz with a double. Standing on second base, Nixon looked into the ecstatic Braves dugout and smiled. It was, he would say later, "a very sweet moment."

Later, after the Braves had claimed a 6–4 victory and a three-games-to-one lead in the series, Nixon stood in front of his locker, bathed in the glare of television lights, and said quietly, "Not being part of it last year makes this mean more to me. I prayed I'd get another chance, that the team would repeat. I don't think anyone wanted to repeat as badly as I did. No fan, no manager, no player."


Deion Sanders left immediately after Game Four and flew by chartered jet to Miami. He arrived at the Falcons hotel at 4:40 Sunday morning, and prepared to play in the team's game against the Dolphins.

What galled the Braves was the manner in which Sanders departed. He informed club president Stan Kasten of his decision to leave Saturday afternoon, after Kasten had telephoned him and demanded to know his plans. Schuerholz still felt Sanders was breaking his word after promising to play with the Braves exclusively through the postseason, but he was helpless to stop him. Furious at Sanders for creating a distraction, Schuerholz admitted he would not have included him on the playoff roster had he known he also planned to play for the Falcons.

"Why would you volunteer to play with twenty-four guys if one guy gets a helmet in the knee?" he asked.

Sanders craves the spotlight. He enjoys being the center of attention. Presented with the opportunity to make history, he couldn't resist, even if it meant breaking his vow to the Braves and risking an injury. That did not sit well with Cox, who admitted he had had his fill of Deion Sanders's Marketing Over America Tour, as one newspaper described it. "I'm tired of it, to be honest with you," he said.

Sanders flew 1,180 miles to don a pair of shoulder pads, pull a black jersey over his head, and play a football game in 87-degree heat. He was in for all but one play on defense, caught a pass on offense, returned four kickoffs and three punts, and made three tackles. He was left exhausted and drained. The Falcons' trainer would not let him go anywhere until they had pumped two bags of intravenous fluids into him, and even then teammate Andre Rison said, "He looks like a piece of you-know-what warmed over."

Then, after receiving the fluids, he hopped a helicopter to Opa-Locka Airport and climbed back aboard the charter jet for the 2-hour-and-20-minute flight to Pittsburgh. By the time Sanders's helicopter landed near Three Rivers and a black limousine whisked him to the stadium, he had just enough time to pull on his uniform, bundle into a parka, and join the Braves in the dugout.

"This is the sort of thing kids dream about," he had said in a CBS interview on the way to Miami. "I'm a kid still."

Cox was asked if he planned to fine Sanders for showing up just before the start of the game. He shook his head and shrugged. "What can I fine him?" he asked. "The man made $118,000 for playing football today."

CBS announcers Tim McCarver and Sean McDonough hammered at Sanders throughout the game for leaving the

Braves. McDonough said he was "self-centered," while Mc-
Carver described him as selfish.

"The guy is playing both ends against the middle," Mc-
Carver said. "They talk about him being the consummate
team player, but if he plays football, what kind of shape will
he be in to play baseball? Why should the income from a shoe
contract take allegiance over the baseball team? The way I see
it, it's flat wrong."

While Cox, Schuerholz, and CBS's finest fumed at Sanders, his teammates rolled their eyes and chuckled. They had
become accustomed to his behavior and didn't seem to mind
his "me first" attitude.

"We all envy his talent," Smoltz said. "We all wish we could
do the same thing. The concern is that he might get hurt and
we couldn't use him off the bench. He's a valuable asset."


Cox decided to stick with his three-man rotation and start
Avery in Game Five, although logic seemed to dictate he give
him an extra day's rest and start Charlie Leibrandt or Pete
Smith. Power pitchers like Smoltz and Avery need four days
off between starts to replenish their fastballs, a schedule that
became especially necessary in this postseason after each
pitcher had already worked more than 230 innings during the
season. Smoltz had not been sharp working on three days rest
in Game Four, and with a two-game advantage in the series,
Cox could afford to add a fourth starter. He had used a four-
man rotation in last year's playoffs, and a well-rested Smoltz
and Avery had each won two games. But Cox wouldn't budge
from his decision to start Avery with three days rest, a decision
he would soon regret.

Avery eagerly anticipated being on the mound when the
Braves won the game that would send them to the World
Series. He had watched Smoltz dance with joy after winning
Game Seven of the playoffs last year and he had seen Lei-
brandt win the division-clinching game in September, and
now he felt it was his turn.

"I had a chance to be on the mound when we won a World

Series last year, but it didn't work out," he said. "I want another chance to be the one holding the ball when we win a championship. That is everybody's dream."

Avery's dream shattered so quickly it took his breath away. His pitches lacked velocity and movement, and the Pirates wasted no time in burying him. They slammed five hits in the first inning, including four doubles, and a crestfallen Avery headed to the showers having given up four runs while recording only one out. After establishing a playoff record in Game Two for consecutive shutout innings, he nearly set another record on this night: His start was the shortest in playoff history since the Pirates' Bob Moose faced five hitters without getting an out in Game Two of the 1972 series.

"I don't really have any explanation," Avery said. "You never think that's going to happen."

As disappointing as Avery's outing was, more ominous from the Braves' perspective was the emergence of Barry Bonds from his postseason doldrums. He and Leyland had met behind closed doors following Game Four for what the manager later termed "a father-son chat." During the conversation, Leyland urged Bonds to relax and start enjoying himself.

"I told Barry, like I told Bobby [Bonilla] last year, he ought to be the happiest guy in the world," Leyland said. "He has a chance to play in a World Series, and then he'll have a chance to make about $30 million. Why should he ever frown? Why should he worry?"

Bonds had emerged from the meeting feeling as if a great weight had been lifted from his shoulders.

"Jimmy is like a gift from heaven," he said.

Bonds left the clubhouse at 2:00 A.M., a relaxed and confident man. That night he strode to the plate in the first inning against Avery and drove home a run with a double, and arrived at second base yelling, "It's over! It's over!" Asked later to explain, he grinned and said, "I didn't understand how a guy could play for 162 games and then disappear for seven games every October. That's why I got to second base and wanted to tell my family and tell Pittsburgh, that the jinx is over."

The Braves seemed dazed by the first-inning bombardment and they never recovered. They managed just three hits against Pirates starter Bob Walk, who had given up the grand slam to Ron Gant in Game Two. They couldn't push a run across the plate until the eighth inning. The Pirates won 7–1 and all the Braves could do afterward was shrug helplessly and search for an explanation.

"Some things happen that you can't explain," Jeff Blauser offered. "And, you shouldn't even try."


The Braves had hoped they wouldn't have to see Tim Wakefield again. However, as the series shifted back to Atlanta for Game Six, that was the unpleasant prospect they faced. They tried to focus their attention elsewhere —"I think a little too much is being made about Wakefield," Blauser said—but it was impossible. They would make a final attempt to solve his unsolvable pitch, and no one was looking forward to the experience. Along with Dal Canton, former Brave and future Hall of Famer Phil Niekro accepted an invitation to throw his knuckler before the game. Niekro hopped a plane from Los Angeles and arrived at Atlanta–Fulton County Stadium just in time to slip into a uniform, borrow spikes and a glove from Jeff Treadway, and head to the mound.

"It was," he joked later, "the first time I've ever gone out there and let them hit the ball."

Niekro was intent on showing the Braves that a knuckleball is hittable, but he was only partially successful. Most of the hitters came away from the batting cage moaning about the pitch and shaking their heads. Later, Niekro would discuss the knuckleball with the Braves and offer them some simple advice. "You have to look for a knuckleball in a particular zone or area," he said. "You don't hit a good knuckleball and if you do it's by luck. [You have to] wait for the one that's bad. Wakefield has got a great knuckleball, but he's going to make some mistakes. You're going to get a pitch to hit. It may not be the first at-bat, but sometime you will get one."

As batting practice ended Wakefield approached Niekro,

who won 318 games during his career, and the two men shook hands.

"I told him he has a great knuckleball," Niekro said. "I'm very impressed with it."

Tom Glavine, who had made 105 pitches in losing Game Three to Wakefield, headed to the mound on three days' rest. Although he had given up just three runs in his previous start, he had not been particularly sharp. His control was a little off, and the shortened rest between starts had not allowed him much time to work on the problem with Leo Mazzone, so he figured to make adjustments during the game. As it turned out, he never got the chance. Like Avery, he experienced one of the worst outings of his career.

A rejuvenated Bonds greeted him with a home run in the second inning. Five more hits followed, the last a three-run homer by shortstop Jay Bell. Before a harvest moon had peeked over the top of the stadium, Glavine knew the game was lost. "I look back and I can't believe how fast it happened," he said later.

Before Cox could wearily climb the dugout steps and head to the mound, the Pirates had scored eight runs and Glavine had not gotten an out in the inning.

"I felt fine, I felt relaxed, but my location was terrible," he said.

Given an enormous lead, Wakefield relaxed and set to work. Justice was the only Brave to figure out the knuckleball; he launched a pair of home runs, driving in three runs, but it was far too little too late. Pittsburgh added four more runs in the fifth, and the crowd began to stream out the exits. By the end of the 13–4 embarrassment, the stands were virtually deserted. "A good old-fashioned butt-whipping" is how Blauser described it. Bewildered, the Braves tried to figure out what had happened and couldn't. Leyland offered the best explanation: "It was just one of those freak nights," he said.

Just three days before, the Braves had held a commanding three-games-to-one lead in the series. Now the series was tied and for a second straight year, the two teams would decide the National League pennant by playing one game.

In a stunned and silent clubhouse, Blauser sat before his locker and offered a grim smile. "We can't afford to sulk about this game," he said. "If you get down in the dumps during the postseason, you're in the wrong business."

Smoltz was smiling and he had a bounce in his step. It was his turn on the mound in another Game Seven and he relished the challenge. "There is something about big games that makes me concentrate and bear down just a little more," he had said earlier in the series. "I really feel as if I should be in them." He and Drabek would oppose each other for the third time in the series. Smoltz had emerged the winner each time and, in fact, had never been beaten in six career postseason starts. Still, the Pirates felt confident about facing him for the third time in nine days, and figured they had history on their side. Pittsburgh had trailed Baltimore three games to one in the 1979 World Series, then won Game Five, and took Games Six and Seven on the road to become world champs. Bonds thought it was time for a repeat performance.

"Finally, we get to meet them face-to-face, they no longer have their backs turned to us," he said. "It's going to be a war."

The Pirates scored in the first inning when Smoltz issued a walk to leadoff hitter Alex Cole, Andy Van Slyke doubled, and Orlando Merced sent a sacrifice fly to Justice in right field. It was an ominous start for the Braves, who had not held a lead since Game Four. Like Smoltz, home plate umpire John McSherry struggled through the first inning. He was suffering from dizziness, and after the Pirates batted in the second inning he left the field and was taken to Piedmont Hospital to be examined. Randy Marsh, who had worked the plate in Game Two, hurried into the umpire's room and slipped on his shin guards and chest protector, and the game resumed.

After pounding on Drabek in his two previous starts, the Braves seemed mesmerized by his pitches. They appeared tight and managed just one hit in the first five innings. Damon

Berryhill was the only player to reach base against Drabek during that stretch. He led off the third inning with a double, but never advanced past second base as Lemke, Smoltz, and Nixon went in order.

Smoltz, who had made 225 pitches in winning Games One and Four, began to tire in the sixth. Bell led off with a double and Van Slyke singled for a 2–0 lead, and Cox began plotting how he'd use the bullpen. In addition to the relievers, he also had Glavine and Avery available, and he had decided he would use them if it became necessary. Smoltz escaped the sixth with no further damage, but he was spent. In the dugout, Mazzone telephoned the bullpen and told Ned Yost to make sure Stanton was ready to pitch the seventh.

Drabek survived his own crisis in the sixth. Lemke singled, and Jeff Treadway, pinch hitting for Smoltz, hit a wedge shot that fell into shallow left field. Nixon, held hitless since Game Four, followed with a perfect bunt. Suddenly the bases were loaded with no outs and the crowd, silent for much of the game, rose to its feet and began to roar. Blauser, with just 1 hit in his last 10 at-bats, approached the plate with one thought in mind: He wanted to lift one of Drabek's pitches to the outfield, deep enough for Lemke to tag up and score from third. At the same time, he also cautioned himself to be selective and not allow Drabek to sucker him into swinging at a pitch that could result in a double-play grounder. Blauser got ahead of him 2-and-1 and guessed Drabek would come next with a fastball. He was right. The ball shot on a line—at third baseman Jeff King, who gloved it and stepped on third, doubling off Lemke, who stood frozen 15 feet down the line.

The roar died in the crowd's throats. They gasped in disbelief. The Braves had seemed certain to score at least one run, probably two, and now the crowd sat deflated, sure the club had already used up its share of miracles. But in the dugout, the Braves were feeling just the opposite. Even as the inning ended with Pendleton's line drive at Bonds in left field, they could sense their resolve strengthening. This was not the end, they told themselves, not by a long shot.

"As each inning went by, you could feel the confidence building," Blauser said. "I don't quite know how to explain it. We kept telling each other that we had come too far to let this slip out of hand. We're too good a team to lose this. Somehow, some way, we have to do it."

Stanton and the bullpen nearly gave Cox a heart attack over the next two innings. The Pirates loaded the bases with two outs in the seventh before Avery was called in to face Van Slyke. He forced a fly to end the threat, then dove right back into trouble the next inning. Bonds singled and Merced bounced a grounder to Blauser, who forced Bonds at second. King followed by roping a double into the right field corner and Merced galloped around the bases and turned for home. Sprinting to the ball, Justice picked it up, whirled, and threw. His throw sailed straight and true, and Berryhill grabbed it and tagged a sliding Merced, whose face fell as Marsh pumped his fist and yelled "Out!" It was a close call for the Braves, who breathed a mighty sigh of relief in the dugout and, looking heavenward, offered up a little prayer of thanks.

Drabek rolled into the ninth inning still leading 2–0. He had allowed just five hits, but after throwing 178 pitches in his two previous starts, and nearly 120 in this game, he was beginning to run out of gas. Pendleton, who had been virtually silent through the entire series, opened by lining a double into right field. The crowd, wanting to believe a final miracle was about to unfold, climbed to its feet and began chanting. Justice strode from the on-deck circle and settled into the box. Drabek let his breath out in a long sigh and glanced into the dugout. Leyland remained rooted in a corner, watchful and anxious. Justice lifted his bat above his head and waved it gently, like a cat twitching its tail, then banged Drabek's pitch hard on the ground to the right of second baseman Jose Lind. Taking quick, sure steps, Lind bent to backhand the ball, just as he had done thousands of times before, and the ball hopped up and sped past him. Lind, who would be named the league's top-fielding second baseman a month later, stared in disbelief at his glove. Flustered, Drabek issued a walk to

Bream, loading the bases, and Leyland finally made his way from the dugout and headed to the mound. Standing next to Bream, first base coach Pat Corrales leaned toward him and said, "Man, Lind never does that. Something is going on here."

Taking the ball from Drabek, Leyland waved in Stan Belinda, an imposing right-hander who delivered the ball with a sweeping sidearm motion. Gant was due next, hitless since he singled in the second inning of Game Four, but Cox was stuck with him after using Treadway and Sanders as pinch hitters earlier in the game. Belinda peered in for the sign from catcher Mike LaValliere and Gant, in a slight crouch at the plate, slammed a high drive toward the left field stands. Pleading for the ball to go out, the crowd noise rose and became deafening. Bonds drifted back and two steps shy of the wall he gloved the ball, and Pendleton tagged at third base and crossed the plate with Atlanta's first run. On the bench, Cox felt a surge of exhilaration as Gant's drive climbed into the night sky. "It has a chance, it has a chance," he thought excitedly. Watching Bonds track the ball, he tempered his disappointment with the realization that the Braves still had the tying run in scoring position with only one out.

The switch-hitting Berryhill was next, and Leyland decided to stick with Belinda. It was a decision he soon regretted. Five pitches, four of them balls, later the bases were loaded again, the tying run on third and pennant-winning run on second, and Hunter approached the plate to bat for Rafael Belliard. Leyland still stayed with Belinda and he got a fastball in on Hunter's hands, forcing a popup to Lind. Two outs. Cox sent Francisco Cabrera to the plate, batting for Jeff Reardon. The happy-go-lucky Dominican who had spent most of the season at Richmond, had collected only 10 at-bats with the Braves in September, and just one in the playoffs. He was considered a mediocre defensive catcher and his skills at first base were average at best, but he could hit. Boy, could he hit. Though he had played no part in the second straight division crown, Cabrera would always be remembered in Braves lore as the player who hit a two-out, three-run homer in the ninth inning against the Reds' Rob Dibble in an August game last year, a hit that propelled Atlanta to a crucial victory. An hour before the start of this game he had been standing along the right field line chatting in Spanish with Carlos Navarro and his wife, Maria, a Cuban couple who lived in an Atlanta suburb, when Carlos suggested, "Why don't you do a repeat of Cincinnati tonight?" Laughing, Cabrera had replied, "All I need, amigo, is a chance."

His opportunity had arrived. Like most Dominican-born players, Cabrera was a free swinger. The expression Dominicans use to describe their style is, "You can't walk off the island." Cabrera was a perfect example. His shiny black bat seemed alive. It wiggled as he held it at a slight angle behind his right ear, and a chaw of tobacco protruded from his cheek. He was a deadly fastball hitter, as Dibble had discovered. Belinda's first pitch was a curve, which swept wide of the plate. He backed off the pitching rubber and walked around the mound. His next pitch zipped high and outside, and the crowd's roar began to shake the stadium. A walk would tie the game. Cabrera knew what was coming next. Belinda would have to throw a fastball, and he would be ready. His bat was poised over his right shoulder. He gazed steadily out at Belinda, and when the fastball arrived he lashed at it, driving it deep into the left field stands—but foul. A sense of anticipation was building in the Braves dugout.

"All of a sudden we looked at each other like, 'Hey, Frankie is going to hit this guy,'" Blauser recalled. "Don't ask us how we knew, we just knew."

Cabrera stood at the plate, ready for another fastball. In the Braves radio booth, broadcaster Skip Caray raised his voice to be heard above the din. Belinda swung into his delivery and a split-second later Cabrera's bat flashed forward. The ball bounced past shortstop Jay Bell and went into left field. Justice scored. As Bonds charged the ball, Bream chugged around third, his face strained and his eyes fastened on the plate.

Bonds's throw was accurate, but high. Bream's toe slid onto the plate just ahead of LaValliere's tag. Later, the catcher would shake his head and moan, "I'm five-foot-eight. If I'm five-foot-eight-and-a-half, he's out." Leaping at Bream and shouting with joy, Justice tumbled on top of him, and he was quickly buried beneath a dozen players.

"David was holding me so tight, I think I turned green and blue," Bream said later. "But it was worth it."

The stadium was bedlam. Andy Van Slyke sank to the ground in center field and watched the celebration numbly. Cabrera disappeared into a surging mass of delirious teammates. "I was just trying to make contact," he recalled later. "The next thing I know I'm at first base and yelling he is safe. I don't remember anything after that. Just that we won and I am the hero. I used to dream about this."

The crowd's roar was thunderous. It continued unabated for 15 minutes. Fans had just witnessed what Stan Kasten would later call "without a doubt, the greatest finish in the history of Atlanta sports," and they refused to leave. Players leaped into each other's arms and danced around the infield in pure, unbridled jubilation. Slowly making his way toward the dugout, Nixon pumped his fist and thought to himself, "This is a gift of God to the Atlanta Braves. It don't get no better."

Pandemonium spread throughout the city. On Peachtree Street, traffic became gridlocked as fans danced in the street and shouted with glee. They spilled from bars to toast the Braves' triumph, they banged on newspaper boxes, and they started singing. The clubhouse was chaotic. Champagne bottles popped and the bubbly flowed in small rivers. "Incredible," Cox said later. "Just incredible." Deion Sanders seized the moment to retaliate for Tim McCarver's critical remarks by dousing him with buckets of water, an act that outraged the broadcaster and prompted him to declare later, "This was an act of cowardice. It was childish and immature. . . . It says a lot about him that this sort of thing is his main thrust after his team just won to reach the World Series." Sanders responded later by saying, "How can you be a coward for throwing water on an individual? The guy didn't want us to win, and we won." Several weeks after the World Series ended, National League president Bill White fined Sanders $1,000 for the incident. He appealed the fine.

While Sanders was busy with his vendetta, the rest of the Braves wept tears of joy. Said Blauser, "What happened to us tonight is what every boy in this country dreams about." Outside the clubhouse, Cox met Leyland and the two men embraced. His face haggard and his jaw trembling, Leyland said, "Congratulations, Bobby, you deserved it." Cox, who counts Leyland among his friends and regards him as one of the finest managers in the game, swallowed hard and replied, "So did you, Jimmy. I don't know what to say."

In the Pirates clubhouse, Bonds sat unmoving on a chair inside his locker. A feeling of shock gripped the room. The Pirates would probably lose Bonds and Drabek to free agency during the winter and everyone knew this would be their best shot at a World Series for many years. One out away from a chance at a world championship, they had watched in horror as Bream, their former teammate, crushed their hopes. It was a devastating loss, and Leyland fought back tears as he faced the television cameras. "This is without question the toughest loss I've ever had to handle," he said. "I felt like that game was ours."

It would be a night the Braves and their fans would never forget. Caray's call of the final play would be heard over and over again during the next few days. *"One run is in, here comes Bream, here's the throw to the plate, he is . . . SAFE! Braves win! Braves win! Braves win! Braves win! Braves win!"* The Braves had completed one of the greatest comebacks in baseball history and it was left to Cabrera to express all their feelings: "This is like a dream come true," he said. "I can't believe it happened."

# THE WORLD SERIES

**Stepping from** the dugout a day before the World Series opened, Bobby Cox was greeted by the sight of hundreds of reporters and television crew members swarming around the batting cage at Atlanta–Fulton County Stadium. It had been two days since Game Seven of the playoffs had ended, and Cox still hadn't caught up on his sleep. Almost as soon as the clubhouse had been cleared of empty champagne bottles and beer cans, he, the coaches, and the scouts had begun plotting strategy against the American League champion Toronto Blue Jays. Cox smiled when he considered playing a team he once managed for baseball's grand prize. "It's special for me," he said. "I managed up there for four years and I love the people. It will be a fun series." Now, before the Braves took batting practice during an hour-long workout in preparation for Game One, Cox was swallowed up by hordes of journalists clamoring for a comment. He repeated the same lines over and over: why he had left Toronto; how delighted he was his old friend, Blue Jays general manager Pat Gillick, had made it to his first World Series; how happy he was for Toronto manager Cito Gaston.

Cox reserved a place in his heart for Toronto. He had headed north of the border after being fired as Braves manager following the 1981 season and became a popular figure in a Blue Jays uniform. He had helped turn a seventh-place team into a contender, and it was there that he experienced the joy of winning a division title for the first time. In four years as manager, he had pushed the team at least one place higher in the standings each season. However, after winning the division title in 1985, the Blue Jays lost the playoffs to the Kansas City Royals after leading three games to one, and they had not come any closer to the World Series until now. It had shocked Toronto and the Blue Jays when Cox accepted the Braves' offer to return to Atlanta as general manager following that '85 season.

"It was the deal of a lifetime," Cox told the gathered media. "To come back to your hometown was something I couldn't pass up. A lot of people don't have the advantage of being able to work and play in the same place. There is so much separation in this game that it's good to be with your family."

His thoughts never strayed far from Toronto, though. He and Gillick talked on the phone regularly, and it was Cox who had brought Gaston onto the Blue Jays coaching staff as hitting coach. When Cox left, Jimy Williams was named manager, and when he was fired 36 games into the 1989 season and joined the Braves organization, Gaston took over and led the team to a division title. Former Blue Jays catcher Buck Martinez, now working on the club's broadcast team, sensed the deep feelings Cox and Gaston carried into the Series.

"It means a lot to Bobby and Cito both," he said. "Cito appreciates Bobby giving him the opportunity to go to Toronto. Bobby recognized his talent as a coach and a leader. It's very emotional for Bobby too."

Cox had rooted for the Blue Jays as they headed down the stretch in a tight race with the Baltimore Orioles in September, then pulled for them in the playoffs. He phoned Gillick from his car after the Blue Jays won and offered his congratulations, then asked him to pass them along to Gaston.

"I was pulling like the devil for Cito to get in there," Cox admitted. "Cito is a great friend of mine."

Cox and Williams weren't the only Braves with ties to the Blue Jays. Francisco Cabrera, Atlanta's newest folk hero, had been signed by Toronto as a free agent in 1985, then traded to the Braves four years later. He still had many friends on the team and was eager to return to the city where he broke into the major leagues. "It will be good to hit against them and see what happens," he said. "I really want to play against the team I used to play for." The past two days had blurred in Cabrera's mind. The day after the hit that delivered the National League pennant, Georgia governor Zell Miller had issued a proclamation.

"I'm not only proclaiming this Francisco Cabrera Day in Georgia," he said, "I'm proclaiming this Francisco Cabrera Year!"

Cabrera found his new celebrity status intoxicating. He had stopped at a local supermarket near his home for some bread and milk the day after Game Seven and was immediately surrounded by shoppers demanding his autograph. Before he could escape, the store manager thrust a fruit basket, a cake, and cookies into his arms. Everywhere Cabrera turned, someone wanted to give him something. He entered a shoe store and walked out with a new pair of shoes. He stopped at a restaurant and was treated to lunch. It dawned on him later that he should have walked into a bank and seen how the tellers responded. *Listin*, the Caribbean's biggest newspaper, carried the headline "The Hit of His Life" to describe his heroics. He couldn't turn on the television without seeing a replay of his hit. He was a hero and he basked in the glory.

"Everywhere I go I have to sign autographs," he said. "I enjoy it. It's the first time I sign so many autographs."

Like Cox, Cabrera was caught in the media's feeding frenzy during Friday afternoon's workout. He was surrounded by reporters and everywhere he went another microphone was thrust into his face. He answered the same question dozens of times, and the smile never left his face. "It feels good," he laughed. "It's something that has never happened to me before."

Despite the distraction Deion Sanders caused by playing two sports in one day during the playoffs, and the commotion he caused during the clubhouse celebration following Game Seven, Cox had decided to keep him on the roster. Sanders had not returned to Cox's good graces; he was simply too valuable to leave behind. Also, Cox knew he would have Sanders's undivided attention in the Series: The Falcons were playing in San Francisco on Sunday and Sanders would be unable to join them.

Kent Mercker had aggravated his sore ribs during the celebration following Game Seven, and Cox replaced him on the roster with David Nied. Mercker was infuriated. He threw twice on the side before Game One, and though he experienced slight pain, he told Cox he could pitch. Cox wasn't buying it. Toronto's roster was heavy with right-handed hitters and he wasn't concerned about losing a left-handed reliever. He also chose to leave Alejandro Pena off the roster; Pena, who had been throwing regularly and felt his elbow was sound, understood Cox's dilemma. Mercker didn't.

"I'm not saying I didn't feel anything, but I don't think I have ever pitched without some pain somewhere," he said. "It's just confusing. I saw it coming. I don't know, it looks like they were just looking for some reason to take me off. It's one thing if I was hurt and couldn't pitch, I would understand it. But it's not my decision. I've got to live with that and it's upsetting. It's not going to be the same sitting and watching."

Cox was angered by Mercker's outburst, but he didn't respond. He explained his decision by saying, "We would have been taking a chance with Kent. The biggest thing is David is healthy." With the roster set, Cox turned his attention to the starting rotation. He would have liked Smoltz to go in the first game so he could make three starts if the Series went seven games, but after pitching Wednesday, he couldn't work on only two days' rest. Cox's decision to start Glavine was born more of necessity than confidence in the left-hander, who had made one solid start in the playoffs and been pounded in his other outing. Although he insisted his cracked rib had healed, he wasn't convincing. Cox wondered which Glavine he would see: the one who had dominated the league for four and a half months, or the one who had been chewed up by the Pirates in Game Six.

Glavine, who had taken it personally when his Cy Young season was described as a fluke and used such comments as motivation, began to smolder again when he read what a disappointment he had been in the playoffs. "I'm sure there are going to be people out there wondering why I'm starting," he said. "But what's important is what I think in my heart, and what this team thinks, and that is, when I go out on the field they have confidence I'm going to win."

Gaston had decided to start right-hander Jack Morris in Game One, the same pitcher who had beaten the Braves in Game Seven of the World Series last October. He had jumped from the Twins to the Blue Jays as a free agent last winter, and had produced a 21–6 record in his first season in Toronto. However, he had not been the same pitcher in the playoffs against Oakland. He lost his only decision and emerged with an unsightly 6.57 earned run average. Still, the Blue Jays considered him their leader.

"He's a man's man—that's probably the best way to put it," Gillick said. "He's kind of a rough guy who doesn't care what people have to say about him. He only wants to win."

Just as they did before Game One against Pittsburgh, the Braves gathered in the clubhouse and listened to a scouting report on Toronto presented by Cox and the coaches. Though Glavine had faced several of the Blue Jays' hitters when they played in the National League, most of their lineup was unfamiliar to him. That gave him an advantage: They were unaccustomed to his style of pitching and his tactics. Even after reading their scouting reports on him, the Blue Jays were unprepared for the changeup that Glavine uses in any situation, the snap of his curve, and the sinking motion of his fastball. "He's a guy you have to see more than one time to hit," Gaston said later.

After former president Jimmy Carter threw out the first ball and both teams were introduced, Glavine strode to the mound and dissected Toronto with a precision that had been missing for six weeks. He knew he was on top of his game in the first inning when he forced ground balls from Devon White, Roberto Alomar, and Joe Carter, an indication that his fastball had returned to his arsenal. His only mistake came in the fourth inning when he tried to bring a fastball in on Carter's hands and the ball strayed out over the plate. Carter smashed it into the left field seats to give the Blue Jays a 1–0 lead.

Meanwhile, Morris had picked up where he left off last October. Using a forkball that approached the plate looking like a fastball before diving sharply, he limited the Braves to Nixon's first-inning single through five. However, he didn't have precise command of his pitches, and the Braves began refusing to swing at the forkballs that dipped around their ankles. He issued consecutive walks to Justice and Bream in the fourth, then gave up another pair of walks the next inning. He was doing a high-wire act and the Braves were waiting for him to slip.

Justice drew a one-out walk in the sixth, Bream singled, and Gant bounced a grounder at shortstop Manuel Lee, who forced Bream at second. There were two outs, a pair of runners on base, and Berryhill was at the plate. He had suffered through a horrible playoff series, hitting just .167, and he was anxious to contribute. Morris got ahead of him 1-and-2, and Berryhill backed away from the plate and scolded himself. "I tried to hit a home run on strike two and missed it badly," he said later. "So I stepped out of the batter's box and told myself, 'Don't try for a home run.' "

Standing on the mound with his eyes narrowed and his mustache bristling, Morris figured to strike him out with a forkball. He had gotten him out in his first two at-bats—a strikeout in the second inning with a forkball, then a soft fly to White in center field in the fifth. Reaching into his glove, he forced the ball between his first two fingers, the grip that would give the pitch the tumbling spin that marked a forkball, then wound up and delivered. He expected the ball to break down and in on Berryhill, who was swinging from the left-hand batter's box, but the pitch stayed up. Berryhill met it with a short, quick uppercut, and the ball rose like a rocket toward the right field stands.

"One bad pitch and the guy didn't miss it," Morris moaned later.

Nearing first base, Berryhill raised a clenched fist over his head as the ball sailed over the wall. Beaming like a little boy who has discovered the bike under the Christmas tree is his, he circled the bases as the crowd's roar enveloped him. "I didn't really feel myself hit the ground until I reached third base," he said. "When you see the ball leave the park—for that one moment—you are on top of the world."

Berryhill's three-run homer was all Glavine needed. He roared through the final three innings, allowing just one man to reach base, and finished with a four-hit complete game. It was sweet vindication for a pitcher who felt he had to keep proving himself, even after back-to-back 20-win seasons.

"To sit here the last three days and read how terrible I've been in the postseason is very aggravating," he said. "It's remarkable how quickly people jump ship. It's as if they threw out the regular season. All they care about is 'What have you done lately?' Did it motivate me? Definitely. I had a burning desire to quiet some of those who doubted me."


Since Ron Gant's grand slam in Game Two of the playoffs his bat had been silent, and Cox decided to bench him. Gant wasn't the sole cause of the offense's depression—Pendleton had hit .233 in the playoffs, Blauser .208—but Cox felt comfortable replacing him with Sanders. If the Blue Jays had started a left-hander instead of right-hander David Cone, he might have decided to replace Gant with Lonnie Smith, but Sanders had had success against Cone in the past; he had faced him 10 times in his brief career and had six hits, while Gant was a .281 career hitter against him. Still, the change came as a surprise. Cox normally didn't pay much attention to a player's statistics against a particular pitcher, but he felt the lineup needed a jolt. Sanders thrived in the spotlight, and Cox was counting on him to ignite the offense, even though he had been to the plate only five times during the playoffs, striking out three times. Cox was playing a hunch and he kept his fingers crossed it would work out.

"I know he hasn't played that much lately, but he's been swinging the bat well in batting practice, so we thought we'd take a chance," he said.

When Gant walked into the clubhouse Sunday afternoon he was shocked to see his name missing from the lineup. He felt it was a slap in the face, a no-confidence vote from the manager. He wanted Cox to stick with him, and he didn't feel it was fair that he was being blamed for the club's offensive woes. "It didn't bother me sitting in the regular season," he said. "But this is the World Series and everyone wants to make the lineup. Bobby is taking his chances. I just hope things work out."

The first controversy of the Series arose before the game even began. A Marine color guard inadvertently carried the Canadian flag upside-down during pregame ceremonies, a slight that outraged Canadians watching on television and caused an international flap that reverberated all the way to the White House. Though the incident wasn't grounds for the missile silos to be opened, it was a major embarrassment, and red-faced baseball officials hastily issued an apology. "It was windy out there and the flag was all furled up because we didn't want it flapping around," explained Wayne Long, a Braves vice-president and director of marketing. "When we saw it unfurl, we all took a deep breath and said, 'Oh, no.' "

Most fans and players at the stadium didn't notice the up- side-down Maple Leaf, but Canadian callers lit up the switchboards at the CTV network in Toronto, and angry fans swamped the offices of the *Toronto Star* newspaper with phone calls. "How could they get the Maple Leaf upside down?" asked one caller. "If someone ever put their flag upside down they would go wrangy."

The Marines were very apologetic. A young soldier, hurrying to get the Canadian flag attached to the pole before the game, had not noticed it was upside down. "Please know it was a mistake and it was not intentional," Sergeant Sandy Wilson of the Sixth Marine Corps District in Atlanta said the next day.

Blauser, grinning, said, "The guy is probably still doing pushups back at his base."

The next day a front-page story in the *Toronto Star* read, "The Maple Leaf simply fell victim to American ignorance."

President Bush apologized. The commandant of the Marine Corps asked that another color guard be allowed to present the Canadian flag before Game Three at Toronto's SkyDome. They did, and this time the Maple Leaf was hung correctly.

The Braves weren't aware of the uproar caused by the upside-down flag; they were too busy focusing on Cone, who had spent his career with the New York Mets before being traded to the Blue Jays in August. He had a lively fastball and a knee-buckling curve, and was leading Smoltz in the league's strikeout race by a wide margin when he was traded. Like Morris the previous night, Cone struggled with his control early in the game. He walked Justice in the second inning, and Justice eventually scored the game's first run on a wild pitch. Another walk, this time to Bream in the fourth, led to another run.

Meanwhile, Smoltz, in his fourth start of the postseason, overwhelmed the Blue Jays. He struck out five of the first six hitters he faced, including consecutive strikeouts of the heart of Toronto's lineup—Dave Winfield, John Olerud, and Kelly Gruber—in the second. In the fourth, some help from home plate umpire Mike Reilly kept the Blue Jays off the scoreboard. Roberto Alomar drew a leadoff walk and was at third base with two out when Smoltz's first pitch bounced in front of the plate, hopped against Berryhill's chest protector, and rolled away. Alomar dashed home and belly-flopped at the plate, sliding a hand underneath Smoltz, who was waiting as Berryhill's throw arrived. He was clearly safe as Smoltz's tag came late, but Reilly called him out, and Gaston charged from the dugout to argue. It was a futile exercise. Reilly had blown the call, but he wouldn't change his decision and both he and Gaston knew it. However, though no one knew it at the time, the play would ripple across the next inning and help shape the game's outcome.

Smoltz had received a scrape on his left wrist when Alomar slid into him, and while the Braves batted, trainers wrapped it with tape. It was a minor injury and he thought no more about it until Gaston strode from the dugout in the fifth inning and pointed out that the tape was a distraction to the hitters. Gaston's complaint was a minor annoyance, but it served to break Smoltz's concentration. He had gotten the first two outs, but after the interruption to change the color of the wrap, he issued a walk to Pat Borders. Manuel Lee followed with a broken-bat single, and Cone slapped a 3-and-2 pitch into center field to score Borders. White tied the game by barely beating out an infield chopper, a grounder that second baseman Mark Lemke bobbled momentarily, allowing Lee to cross the plate.

But just as quickly as they had tied the game, the Blue Jays found themselves trailing by two runs again as Cone could not last the fifth inning. Sanders singled and stole second, Pendleton walked, and Justice drove a single into right field for a 3–2 lead. Bream followed with a sacrifice fly, and the crowd began its familiar chant, the sound rolling across the field and sending chills dancing along everyone's spine.

"The fans are like a tenth man," Blue Jays bench coach Gene Tenace said later. "If I was on that team, it would give me a little extra adrenaline flow. The fans add another dimension."

Smoltz carried a 4–2 lead into the eighth inning before he tired. Alomar doubled with one out, Carter singled, and Winfield pulled the Blue Jays to within one run with another base hit. With the left-handed-hitting Olerud next, Cox decided that was all for Smoltz. He waved in Stanton, who forced a popup for the second out. Again, Cox ambled out of the dugout and headed to the mound. He liked playing the percentages, and he wanted a right-hander to face the right-handed-hitting Gruber. Reardon walked in slowly from the bullpen and accepted the ball. The strategy worked, as Gruber was caught looking at a third strike, leaving runners stranded on the corners.

Cox felt the tension begin to ease in the dugout. It was just this situation that Schuerholz had in mind when he had traded for Reardon: a tight game in the postseason, the Braves clinging to a slim lead, and the ninth inning looming. Reardon stood on the mound in the ninth needing just three outs for the Braves to take a commanding two-games-to-none lead in the Series. He got Borders to line out to Justice, then ran the count full to Derek Bell, hitting for Lee. His next pitch was low and Bell trotted to first base as Toronto's dugout came alive. The pitcher's slot in the batting order was due next and Gaston scanned his bench. He had already used Candy Maldonado, who had hit .272 with 20 homers during the season, as a pinch hitter in the seventh inning. His eyes fell on Ed Sprague, a young catcher who had spent most of the season in the minors, and had gotten just two at-bats in the playoffs. Gaston motioned for him to grab a bat. Before the inning started, Sprague thought he might get a chance to hit. Since he hadn't seen Reardon before, he sat and watched how the veteran reliever approached the Blue Jays.

"He threw some high fastballs and somebody said to look for something down," he said later. "I went up there looking for something I could stay on top of."

Braves scouts had watched Sprague during the final two weeks of the season and had noted he was an excellent low fastball hitter. Their reports suggested throwing breaking pitches to him and using fastballs up and in. That fit neatly with Reardon, who had spent his career throwing high fastballs past hitters. Berryhill signaled for a fastball and Reardon aimed for the letters on Sprague's uniform top. The pitch sped to the plate and Reardon watched, horrified, as it stayed low. Sprague swung and the crack of his bat silenced the crowd. The ball climbed into the left field stands so quickly Sprague wasn't even sure it had gone out. He circled the bases, stunned, then fell into the arms of his frenzied teammates.

"All-time saves leader. Boom. First pitch," Winfield described later. "He can hit. They didn't know it, but they know it now."

Reardon got the final two outs, and as he left the mound his face was a mask of despair. He walked slowly toward the dugout, his shoulders slumped and his heart heavy. "It's pretty tough for this to happen in a World Series game," he said later. The Braves threatened Blue Jays closer Tom Henke in the bottom of the inning, putting two men on base with two outs, but they had exhausted their supply of miracle finishes. Pendleton lifted a popup to Gruber, who circled into foul ground to glove it and end the game.

The Braves were subdued in their clubhouse. They had been two outs away from taking firm control of the Series and now they faced the prospect of playing the next three games in Toronto's SkyDome. Cox, shaking his head, his voice low, said, "You get upset when you lose like that. It hurts any time that happens." Now the Braves knew a little of how the Pirates had felt after losing Game Seven of the playoffs. They had been beaten by a third-string catcher who had hit only five homers in the majors before his at-bat in the ninth inning.

"That's just the way it is in the World Series," Roberto Alomar said. "Sometimes little guys do big things."


John Smoltz turned his face upward, gazed in wonder at SkyDome, and whistled softly. It wasn't a stadium, he thought

to himself, it was a palace. The Braves shared Smoltz's amazement. If baseball has to be played indoors, they agreed, it
might as well be in a magnificent structure like SkyDome. A
Hard Rock Café was built into the right field concourse. Hotel
rooms overlooked center field. The stadium was huge and
airy, unlike Minnesota's Metrodome, with its Hefty Bag
fences and off-white ceiling.

"The SkyDome is a real dome, a baseball dome," Smoltz
said. "I don't know what they play in the Metrodome, but it's
not baseball."

Avery would start Game Three and he was determined to
recapture the magic he'd displayed in the 1991 playoffs. The
debacle in Game Five against the Pirates still rankled him,
and like Glavine, he had begun to hear criticism of his postseason performance. "I know the criticism fired Tommy up
and hopefully it'll do the same for me," he said.

The next three games would be played under American
League rules, which meant the Braves would use a designated
hitter. Cox chose Lonnie Smith and inserted him into the
fifth slot in the order, behind Justice. He also decided to give
another start to Sanders, who had reached base three times in
Game Two, stolen two bases, and scored a run. Gant would
sit out another game and he was unhappy. "This is not easy
on him and it's not easy on me," Cox said. "If I was him I'd
be upset, too. He wants to play, but he's a team man first."

Although Sanders had helped spark the offense in Game
Two, he had failed to ignite Pendleton, who continued to flail
helplessly at the plate. He had finished the season tied with
Andy Van Slyke for the league lead in hits, but he had produced just eight, six of them singles, in 37 at-bats in the postseason. A proud man, he knew he was letting his teammates
down, and he became anxious at the plate. "No excuses, no
alibis," Pendleton said. "I'm swinging at bad pitches, pressing
a little. I have to discipline myself. I have to regain a feel for
the strike zone."

Toronto's reluctant starter would be Juan Guzman, a hard-
throwing right-hander who had admitted he didn't particu-

larly care for the pressure-filled games of the postseason. He grimaced when it was mentioned that more than 50,000 fans would fill SkyDome for Canada's first World Series game. He would be the center of attention, the Blue Jays' hopes pinned on him, and he wasn't eager for the opportunity. "I don't like to be in that situation," he admitted. "The situations I've been in the last two times—you know I pitched the [pennant] clinching game—you have a lot of pressure on yourself. I don't like it, but when I don't have any other choice, I just work hard, prepare myself for the game, and do my best." Despite his lack of enthusiasm for big games, Guzman had been Toronto's best postseason pitcher during the last two years. He had won his only start against the Twins in the 1991 playoffs, then he beat Oakland twice in this year's playoffs.

It was important for the Braves to get ahead of Guzman early and swing the momentum to their side. That would help ease the pressure on Avery and relax the hitters. Sanders did his part, singling and stealing second in the first inning, but Pendleton bounced out weakly, Justice struck out, and he was left at third base. He led off the fourth inning with another single, Pendleton followed with a soft hit into right field, and suddenly Guzman looked shaky. It was Justice's turn. He clobbered a fastball, driving it to the deepest part of center field, and Pendleton took one look at it and raced for second base. Center fielder Devon White reacted at the crack of the bat. He whirled and sprinted for the wall, his head cocked and his eyes glued to the ball. As he crossed the warning track at full speed, he leaped and gloved the ball, then crashed into the wall.

"I think the only players who could have made that catch are Andy Van Slyke and Devon," Nixon said later. "I don't know if I could have done it. This is Devon's home and he knows the park."

Pendleton didn't keep his eyes on White. Convinced Justice had a double, he sped around second base and was astonished to see Sanders retreating to tag up. The two players passed each other and second base umpire Bob Davidson immediately ruled Pendleton out. "I never thought White would catch it," Pendleton said later. "I turned one way to look at the ball, then I turned the other way and Deion was passing me." White returned the ball quickly to the infield and Sanders, confused by Pendleton's sprint back to first and unable to hear Davidson's call, raced toward third and was trapped in a rundown. As the Blue Jays infielders converged on him, he scrambled back to second as third baseman Kelly Gruber dove and tagged his ankle. Shockingly, with the play right in front of him, Davidson blew the call. He ruled Sanders safe, foiling the second triple play in Series history, the first since 1920. Later, after seeing replays and newspaper photos of Gruber's tag, Davidson admitted he had erred. "When I first called the play, I thought I was one hundred percent right," he said. "It was right there, it was right in front of me. Then I saw the replays and the pictures, and I thought I probably missed the play. No one feels worse than I do. I don't like to miss plays." The Braves' threat, which moments before had seemed so promising, faded away as Guzman struck out Smith.

Finally, in the sixth, the Braves bunched three hits together and scored a run. Sanders doubled, Pendleton reached on an infield hit, and Justice drove a single past Olerud's dive at first base. Guzman refused to crumble. Using a 95-mph fastball and a hard slider, he got ahead of Smith and forced a fly, then got Bream to bounce out. That raised Atlanta's total to five men left on base, three in scoring position. The game was tied 1–1 in the eighth when Nixon lined a Guzman pitch off Gruber's glove, then stole second. With two outs, Gaston signaled Guzman to walk Justice, bringing Smith to the plate for the third time with a runner in scoring position. This time he delivered, punching a single into left field to score Nixon with the go-ahead run.

Reclaiming his postseason dominance, Avery marched through seven innings, yielding just one run while striking out eight on his way to a season-high total of nine. He had made the same mistake to Joe Carter that Glavine did in Game One. Attempting to get ahead of him with a fastball in the bottom of the fourth, his pitch caught too much of the plate and Carter hammered it into the left field bleachers. He didn't allow another hit until Gruber batted in the eighth inning. Toronto's third baseman was experiencing a nightmarish postseason. He was hitless in 23 consecutive at-bats, and he began to wonder what the record was for futility in the play-offs and World Series. Avery had gotten him on a comeback grounder in the third inning, then walked him in the fifth. Now, as he stood at the plate in a slight crouch leading off the Blue Jays' eighth, Gruber reminded himself not to help Avery, to make him throw strikes. The count ran full and Avery, guessing Gruber was looking for a fastball, threw a changeup. He wanted the pitch to fade down and away, but it split the plate, and Gruber sent it on a high arc over the left field wall.

"Even at 0-for-23, I felt great at the plate," Gruber said later. "But it was a load off my mind to hit the homer."

The scene was set for another stirring finish. Gaston decided to pull Guzman after he had made 116 pitches in eight innings. He called in right-hander Duane Ward, whose usual role was as a setup man for Henke. The Braves seemed ready to claim the lead in the game and the series when Sid Bream led off the ninth with a base hit. A bunt should have followed, but Cox decided to gamble. He sent Hunter in as a pinch runner for Bream and allowed Blauser, who had struck out twice and grounded back to the mound in his three previous at-bats, to swing away. Ward ran the count full and Cox decided to gamble again. He flashed the steal sign to third base coach Jimy Williams and Hunter broke for second as Ward delivered his pitch. Blauser checked his swing, catcher Pat Borders rifled the ball to Alomar, and Hunter was tagged out. The question was, had Blauser swung or not? Home plate umpire Joe West appealed to first base umpire Dan Morrison, who raised his fist and declared a third strike on Blauser.

Cox went berserk. He picked up a batting helmet and angrily flung it at the top step of the dugout. His aim was off. The helmet skittered onto the field and West ejected him. Later, Cox would admit, "I should have been thrown out," but at the time he was too angry to care. He is rarely thrown out of a game, and when he is, he gets his money's worth with the offending umpire. He waved his arms and shouted at West, color rising in his face, and he stomped around in a tantrum. Finally, he retreated to the tunnel leading from the dugout to the clubhouse, out of sight of the umpires, and he managed the bottom of the ninth inning from there.

Avery went out for the ninth and immediately got into trouble. Alomar led off with a single, then took advantage of the left-hander's high leg kick and stole second. Cox's mind was whirling. He ordered Williams to the mound to remove Avery. Mark Wohlers was called in and instructed to intentionally walk Joe Carter. Winfield followed with a bunt, leaving runners on second and third with one out. Williams hurried back to the mound and waved in Mike Stanton to face the left-handed-hitting Olerud, but Gaston outflanked Cox by sending Sprague to the plate as a pinch hitter. Cox was forced to order Sprague intentionally passed, and Williams headed to the mound for a third time. Stanton departed and Reardon arrived.

Candy Maldonado was next. A mediocre player with the Dodgers and Giants, he had gone to the American League and become a star. A chunky, right-handed hitter, he was hitless in seven at-bats in the Series, including four strikeouts. Reardon threw him two sliders and he swung and missed each by a foot. Hoping to get either a strikeout or a ground ball for a double play, Reardon tried a third slider, but it didn't have the same bite, and Maldonado reached out and poked it into center field, over the head of the drawn-in Nixon. Alomar trotted across the plate with the winning run, and the Blue Jays had a two-games-to-one lead in the Series.

"This is the worst thing that has ever happened to me in my career," Reardon said glumly. "This is the World Series and I've let these guys down. I just hope we can come back and win three. Otherwise, I'm going to be thinking about it an awful lot in the off-season."

The Braves were shocked. After winning the playoffs with

one of the most amazing finishes in baseball history, they thought they were destined to become world champions. The Blue Jays were spoiling the party.

"I think we would all rather have it the easy way, but I guess faith has put it where we always have to play with our backs to the wall," Pendleton sighed. "Things don't come easy to a lot of people and I think that's true of the Braves."


The Braves' offensive drought was severe and was about to get worse. With Blue Jays left-hander Jimmy Key scheduled to start Game Four, Cox returned Gant to the lineup and started Hunter at first base for the first time in the Series. Key faced a daunting task: The Braves' order was stacked with eight right-handed or switch hitters; Justice's bat was the only left-handed one in the lineup. Cox had tilted the odds in Atlanta's favor about as much as he could. If the offense didn't come alive now, he was out of options.

The game began promisingly with Nixon's leadoff single, but almost as quickly he was back in the dugout, cursing. He had been warned of Key's pickoff move, but he was still caught leaning, and first baseman John Olerud slapped a tag on his hand. Blauser followed with another single and stole second, but Pendleton and Smith went out, and the Braves shook their heads ruefully, knowing they had blown a great opportunity to seize momentum and shift the pressure into the Blue Jays' dugout.

Key changed tactics in the second inning. He shelved his fastball and began throwing his curve and changeup, keeping the pitches down and working the outside half of the plate. The Braves fell like tenpins. Key retired 14 straight hitters and slowly the life ebbed from the Braves dugout. Justice would cause an uproar the next day when he criticized the team for its lack of spirit. During his regular show with an Atlanta radio station he said, "Our bench was dead. It looked like guys just showed up for a game, a spring training game. The mood from the beginning of the game seemed like the guys were not totally into it. The way it appeared before the game was the enthusiasm was not ever there."

Unknowingly, Sid Bream strengthened Justice's comments in an interview. He said, "I know that each one of our players is giving 110 percent right now. But it seems like . . . I truly believe there are two different ways of going out on the ball-field. You can get excited about playing, but you also have to have the right kind of mindset, the right kind of focus. I think that's where we're lacking."

Making his second start of the Series, Glavine also noticed the lack of enthusiasm. Normally as placid as a Sunday school teacher, he entered the dugout after innings yelling at the top of his voice in an attempt to shake his teammates from their doldrums. "I was just trying to get things going and get some life in the dugout," he said later. "I did that three or four innings, but it didn't seem to work." The Braves fell behind 1–0 in the third when Pat Borders lofted one of Glavine's changeups along the left field line and dropped it into the foul net for a home run. In the seventh, Glavine pitched too cautiously to Gruber, whose home run in Game Three remained his only hit of the Series, and walked him. It was a small mistake, but it proved to be a critical one, because Gruber eventually scored on Devon White's two-out single. Those would be the only runs Glavine would allow, but it would be just enough for the Blue Jays.

The Braves couldn't muster any offense against Key, a .500 pitcher during the season. Nixon was the only man to reach base between the second and eighth innings, and his two-out hit in the sixth was wasted when Blauser grounded into a fielder's choice. When Key finally began to tire in the eighth, the Braves couldn't take advantage. Gant opened the inning with a double and Hunter followed with a bunt single, bringing Berryhill, who did not have a hit since his three-run homer in Game One, to the plate. A bunt was in order, and again Cox disdained the conservative approach. But Berryhill had different ideas. Seeing Hunter catch the Blue Jays unawares with a bunt, he decided he'd give it a try. As Cox and the Braves watched in horror, he stabbed at Key's pitch and lifted a feeble popup to Borders. Cox said later, "I have no idea what was going through Damon's mind," and Berryhill could only offer a helpless shrug and say, "I've attempted it a few times and never popped up. Tonight it was the worst thing that could happen."

With all that had gone wrong for the Braves, they shouldn't have been surprised by Berryhill's failure. Even when they received a break, they couldn't take advantage. After Gant crossed the plate on a Lemke grounder, pulling the Braves to within one run, Nixon was at the plate with two outs to face reliever Duane Ward. He swung and missed Ward's two-strike pitch, but the ball got past Borders and Nixon reached base. That left it up to Blauser to deliver a clutch hit, but he failed again, grounding out weakly. "Right now we should be up three games," Justice said later. "We have been beating ourselves. I'll give the Blue Jays credit, but we have been fighting against ourselves, too, and that has been the whole story."

The heart of the order—Pendleton, Smith, and Justice—fell without a struggle in the ninth, and suddenly, shockingly, the Braves were perched on the brink of elimination. Glavine sat for a long time in a deserted dugout afterward, the expression on his face a mixture of resignation and dismay.

"I felt disappointed more than anything else," he said. "Disappointed and frustrated. It was all going through my mind. I just kind of sat there and hoped we wouldn't go through what we did last year."


The meeting in the Braves clubhouse before Game Five was short and not so sweet. "We knew it was do-or-die night," Lonnie Smith said later. "A couple of guys spoke up. We figured, if we lose it, let's at least give them a game." It was the offense's fault the Braves found themselves trailing three games to one. Collectively, they were hitting .185 and Berryhill's home run in Game One remained their only homer. Blauser was hitting .133. Gant and Justice were at .167.

Lemke, last year's World Series hitting star, was at .154. Nixon and Pendleton were hitting .188.

"Something ain't right," Nixon said. "They aren't hitting either, but they're getting the big hits."

Olson figured he had the answer. He was sitting in his hotel room that afternoon when he received a phone call from the American SIDS Institute in Atlanta. He had exchanged his cast for a smaller, lighter one before the team left for Toronto, leaving the bigger one for the Institute to auction off, but now it was being returned. "They told me it was a good luck cast and it would be on the two o'clock flight," he said. The cast was delivered to the clubhouse a half-hour before the start of the game and it wound up in the dugout, where several Braves took turns rubbing it for luck.

It seemed to work. The Braves scored a run in the first inning for the first time in the Series, added another on Justice's homer in the fourth, then exploded against Blue Jays starter Jack Morris the next inning. It started innocently enough with Nixon's two-out single and stolen base. Sanders, starting in place of Gant again, lined another hit into center field for a 3–2 lead, and Pendleton followed with a double. Gaston ordered Justice walked, loading the bases for Smith. But Morris, unbeatable in the 1991 World Series, had fallen back to earth with a resounding thud. He had hung a forkball to Berryhill to lose Game One, and he decided he wouldn't make that mistake again, so he delivered a fastball, and Smith launched a high drive toward the right field wall. Watching the ball climb toward the roof as right fielder Joe Carter retreated, Smith screamed, "Get out of here, get out of here." Carter backed up as far as he could and watched the ball sail into the Braves bullpen, where reliever Marvin Freeman and catcher Javier Lopez danced an impromptu jig.

Smith circled the bases feeling a sense of satisfaction. Though he knew he could never erase his baserunning blunder in Game Seven of last year's World Series, his grand slam would help soften the memory. "People brought it [the baserunning gaffe] up all the time," he said. "Some called it one of the biggest blunders in World Series history, but whether I felt retribution—no. What I knew was that we had a good lead and the players were a lot more confident."

That was all Olson needed to see. He retired the cast, hopeful the Braves had not used up all its magic. Smoltz took it from there. He would remain unbeaten in nine career postseason starts, limiting the Blue Jays to five hits and a pair of runs in six innings. "Don't ever count this team out, no matter how bad it looks," Nixon said.

A Toronto newspaper had published a proposed parade route that morning in anticipation of a Blue Jays celebration. It was just the thing to fire up a visiting team needing a jolt of enthusiasm. "They may wind up having a parade around here, but it'll be a few days away," Blauser said.


The red, white, and blue bunting hanging from the Atlanta–Fulton County Stadium grandstand rippled in a cool fall breeze. While the Braves had been impressed with SkyDome, there was no place like home. "We have felt all along that if we just could get back to Atlanta, then we could do something about this thing," Nixon said. Avery would have that opportunity in Game Six. He would be matched against Cone, who had lasted only four and a third innings in Game Two.

The Braves attempted to gain the upper hand before the game started. In Toronto, the Blue Jays had played rock-and-roll music over the public address system while they hit in batting practice, then replaced it with elevator music when the Braves took their turn in the cage. Turnabout was fair play: When the Blue Jays' batting practice started, the voice of late opera star Mario Lanza singing "Be My Love" serenaded them as they swung. Placido Domingo followed with the equally uplifting "O Sole Mio," and then "The Itsy-Bitsy Spider" and "Over the Rainbow" came wafting over the loudspeakers.

It didn't seem to bother the Blue Jays, who grabbed a 1–0 lead in the first inning after Devon White singled and eventually scored when Justice misplayed Carter's line drive. Sanders helped the Braves tie the game in the third when he doubled, stole third, and scored on Pendleton's sacrifice fly. But working on three days' rest again, Avery wasn't sharp. He survived the third inning by getting Carter to ground out and Winfield to loft a fly, stranding Alomar at third, but yielded a leadoff homer to Maldonado the next inning. Cox decided he had seen enough of Avery. Pete Smith came on to start the fifth, and he worked the next three innings without giving up a run.

Meanwhile, Cone hung on through six innings by escaping several jams with strikeouts. He got Avery swinging in the second, leaving runners on the corners, then struck out Pendleton to end the fifth with men on second and third. Feeling he had gotten all he could from Cone, Gaston pulled him after six innings and turned a 2–1 lead over to a bullpen that had not given up a run in the series. Todd Stottlemyre, David Wells, and Duane Ward carried the Blue Jays to the ninth inning, and closer Tom Henke was called in to get the final three outs.

Bottom of the ninth, down by a run. It was not an unfamiliar predicament for the Braves. They had spent so much time with their backs against the wall that it was becoming a comfortable position. Olson, who had brought his good-luck cast along to the dugout, wondered if they had one more miracle left. "I was praying," he admitted later. The crowd rose and began to roar as Blauser punched a single into left field. Berryhill got a bunt down, moving Blauser to second base, and Lonnie Smith, pinch hitting for Lemke, drew a walk. The crowd's voice became deafening as Francisco Cabrera, the playoff hero, moved from the dugout. He had not batted since lining that bottom-of-the-ninth single against the Pirates in Game Seven, and now he was being asked to deliver another fantastic finish. He almost did. His line drive bolted into left field and Maldonado, stumbling backward, made an awkward, leaping catch, causing Gaston's heart to jump into his throat.

Nixon stood at the plate as the Braves' last hope. Henke

quickly got ahead of him with two strikes, then he delivered a low fastball that Nixon chopped to the left side of the infield. Third baseman Kelly Gruber took three quick steps to his left, shortstop Manuel Lee darted to his right, but the ball plunged through the hole and rolled into left field. The Braves dugout exploded as Blauser touched home plate with the tying run. Ninety feet separated them from another miracle finish. Smith stood on third base as Gant, who had pinch hit for Sanders in the seventh, settled into the batter's box and waved his bat menacingly above his head. Benched for much of the Series, he had collected just seven at-bats, had one hit, and had not driven in a run. Henke wound up and delivered, and the roar from the crowd faded as Gant lifted a fly to White in center to send the game into extra innings.

Cox turned to Charlie Leibrandt in the tenth inning. Like Lonnie Smith, he had a chance to banish his own World Series nightmare, the memory of Kirby Puckett's home run in the eleventh inning of last year's Game Six. He got through the tenth and watched from the dugout as Henke and left-hander Jimmy Key set the Braves down in order in the bottom of the inning.

Leibrandt walked to the mound in the eleventh with his ghost not far behind. He got the first out, then hit White with a pitch. Alomar singled, and Reardon got up in the Braves bullpen and began to throw. Carter was next and he sent a fly to Nixon in center for the second out. In the dugout, Cox considered his options. With Winfield at the plate, it made sense to call in Reardon, but he had been burned twice before by using him and he hesitated to wave him in again. Later, Cox would say he planned for Reardon to pitch the twelfth. Approaching Winfield cautiously, Leibrandt ran the count full and decided to throw a changeup. "I felt I had to go with my best pitch," he explained later. "I know he's looking for it and he knows it's coming. It's a matter of executing."

Leibrandt didn't get the pitch where he wanted it, sinking down and away. It hung softly in the middle of the plate and Winfield pounced on it, driving it down the left field line.

White scored and Alomar sped home, giving the Blue Jays a 4–2 lead.

Once again the Braves were asked to provide a phenomenal finish and once more it was Blauser who got things started. He lined a single against Key to open the bottom of the eleventh, and Berryhill came to the plate representing the tying run. The crowd groaned as he sent a grounder toward shortstop Alfredo Griffin, but unbelievably, the ball took a strange hop and Griffin flubbed it. "It was the perfect double-play ball and when I saw that go through, I thought, 'Oh, no, here we go again,' " Key said. "I couldn't believe it." Rafael Belliard advanced the runners with a bunt, leaving the task of providing the latest miracle to Hunter. He didn't deliver a hit, but he did bring Blauser across the plate by bouncing a grounder to Carter at first base, also moving Berryhill to third.

Nixon swung a bat in the on-deck circle as Gaston strode to the mound and called in right-hander Mike Timlin. Gaston wanted the switch-hitting Nixon to bat left-handed; he was hitting .400 from the right side, .286 from the left in the postseason. As Gaston turned and departed, Borders reminded Timlin that the scouting report on Nixon described how frequently he bunts.

Nixon, who had bunted safely 17 times during the season, tried again. He met Timlin's pitch and dragged it toward first base. He wanted the ball to squirt down the line, but it angled away, and Timlin, hurrying over, picked it up and flipped it to Carter. For just a moment, Borders, who would be named the MVP, couldn't believe the Series was over. "After the last out, I stood there for a few seconds and said, 'Did we really win?' " he recalled later. Carter leaped off the bag with a shout of joy as the Blue Jays poured from the dugout to surround Timlin and Borders, a scene all too reminiscent of the Braves' celebration 10 days before.

"I'm almost speechless," Winfield said later in the clubhouse. "I can't even think of the words to describe it. This is the most fun I've had playing professional ball."

Down the tunnel from a visitors' clubhouse gone wild, the

Braves were a subdued group. Realizing it was a game they could have won, should have won, the Braves mourned the end of great expectations. Instead of being crowned world champs, they were saddled with another World Series loss, the first team to lose consecutive Series since the Dodgers in 1977–78. The legacy of a memorable season was washed away in the tears of defeat. The Braves moved numbly through the clubhouse, hardly believing their season had ended so suddenly. "Things just happen," Lemke said softly. "We've got to remember the positive things. There's nothing for us to feel down about."

Sitting in a corner of the dugout as the game ended, Leibrandt could only shake his head and reflect on fate's choice of him to emerge the goat again. "I almost pitched well enough," he said sadly. "If I make a little better pitch, who knows what happens. It's going to be a tough winter ahead."

# EPILOGUE

**Terry Pendleton** still felt numb. Rising the morning after Game Six, he couldn't believe it was all over, that the season had ended with another extra-inning loss in the World Series, just as it had in 1991. But the feeling was different this time. Even after losing to the Twins in Game Seven last year, he had felt a sense of pride in what the Braves accomplished. Now, all he felt was despair. It wasn't enough for the Braves to reach the Series again. They were meant to win it and hadn't. A season of high hopes and expectations had evaporated as quickly as Dave Winfield's double had skipped down the third base line in the eleventh inning of the finale. Pendleton knew it would be a long winter filled with painful memories.

It hurt more this year because he had not contributed offensively. After hitting .311 during the season and driving in more than 100 runs for the first time in his career, he hit just .240 against the Blue Jays and drove in two runs. Reflecting back on the six games, he could remember a half-dozen times he had been at the plate in a dramatic situation and had been unable to provide a clutch hit. "Believe me, it weighs heavy on my mind," he said.

Many players play their entire careers without ever reaching a World Series. Pendleton had now played in four Series —and lost each time. At age 32, troubled by aching knees and feeling he was on the downside of his career, he was fearful he would never win a world championship. "That third time's a charm stuff is a bunch of crap," he said. Feeling restless and irritable at home, and needing to be alone, Pendleton jumped into his car and headed for the highway. Later, he would be unable to recall exactly where he went. He drove aimlessly, allowing images of the Series to replay in his mind's eye, reviewing each game pitch by pitch. "I took it personally when I thought about it," he said. "I thought about how terrible I was. I felt like I didn't do my job. When I was needed, I didn't do it."

Scenes flashed through his mind in painful sequence: Ed Sprague's ninth-inning homer in Game Two. Candy Maldonado's two-strike hit to win Game Three. Devon White's bouncing single, scoring the go-ahead run in the seventh inning of Game Four. Maldonado's fourth-inning homer in Game Six. White being hit by Charlie Leibrandt's pitch in the eleventh inning. Finally, he saw Winfield's two-out grounder hug the line and scoot past him, and he experienced the same sense of helplessness he had felt as he watched White and Roberto Alomar round the bases and speed toward home plate with the runs that would give the Blue Jays the championship. "It hurt," he said later. "I think it will hurt for a long time."

Three days after the Series ended, the Braves gathered a final time at Atlanta–Fulton County Stadium for a ceremony honoring their season. A year earlier they had come together for a triumphant ride down Peachtree Street, saluted by 750,000 people and showered with ticker tape; now they would say their good-byes to 26,000 fans waving foam rubber tomahawks. The city did its best to ease the team's disappointment. A red carpet led from the dugout to a stage erected behind second base, and cheerleaders formed a line along the path. Marching bands filled the outfield. A color guard bore the flags of each state into the stadium and Little Leaguers gathered on the infield. A festive spirit hung in the cool afternoon air. The Braves wore smiles in greeting the crowd, but in the clubhouse their grins faded and hurt and disappointment filled their eyes.

"For me, everything was all right until I saw the Blue Jays jumping around at their parade," Tom Glavine said. "That's when it hit me. There you are at the brink of realizing a goal and you don't do it. It's very disappointing."

As the clubhouse slowly emptied, some players departed with a sense of regret, others with a feeling of being set free. In the coming weeks, Alejandro Pena, Lonnie Smith, Jeff Reardon, and Mike Bielecki would become free agents. Pena and Smith would sign with the Pirates, Bielecki with the Indians. Jeff Treadway and Tommy Gregg would be released; Treadway would sign with the Indians, Gregg with the Reds. David Nied, Armando Reynoso, and Vinny Castilla would be lost in the expansion draft. Charlie Leibrandt would be traded to the Texas Rangers. But that lay ahead. Right now, Marvin Freeman was wondering what the future held. As he turned for the door, John Schuerholz crossed the clubhouse floor and extended a hand.

"Good-bye, Marvin, it was a great season," he said.

"And . . ." Freeman replied.

Puzzled, Schuerholz thought for a moment, then his face brightened.

"And, we'll see you next spring," he said.

"All right!" Freeman said. "That's what I wanted to hear."